Interethnic Communication

Interethnic Communication

E. LAMAR ROSS, EDITOR

Southern Anthropological Society Proceedings, No. 12
Gwen Kennedy Neville, Series Editor

The University of Georgia Press
Athens 30602

Southern Anthropological Society

Founded 1966

Library of Congress Cataloging in Publication Data

Main entry under title:
Interethnic communication.
   (Southern Anthropological Society proceedings;
no. 12)
   Papers originally presented as the key symposium of
the 1977 annual meeting of the Southern Anthropological
Society in Miami, Fla.
   1. Intercultural communication—Congresses.
2. Ethnicity—Congresses. I. Ross, E. Lamar.
II. Series: Southern Anthropological Society.
Proceedings; no. 12.
GN2.S9243 no. 12 [GN496]   301.2s [301.2′1]   77–27456
ISBN 0–8203–0441–7
ISBN 0–8203–0442–5 pbk.

Contents

Preface

This volume represents several different approaches to the study of interethnic communication and to the application of knowledge in solving problems of communication breakdown. Some authors deal exclusively with analytical questions, while others address themselves explicitly to the everyday difficulties of living in an ethnic neighborhood, of organizing communities, or of facilitating interpersonal communication across cultural boundaries. The goal of this collection was to assemble statements from scholars and practitioners of diverse backgrounds who would attack the topic of interethnic communication at all levels—in terms of the person, bounded groups, linguistic and racial enclaves, and the nation-state—with the various tools of the social sciences. The result is a collage of studies ranging from the abstract analysis of a mathematical sociologist through the contributions of linguists, communication scientists, political, economic, and other cultural anthropologists, to the personal testimony from a community organizer on the practical aspects of understanding ethnicity.

Papers in this volume were originally presented as the key symposium of the 12th annual meeting of the Southern Anthropological Society in Miami, Florida, in March 1977. Lamar Ross served as organizer of this symposium and is responsible for assembling this varied assortment of contributions on the conference theme. The University of Georgia Press has continued its past history of assistance and support in bringing the SAS Proceedings forth each year.

Gwen Kennedy Neville
SAS Proceedings Editor

Interethnic Communication

Interethnic Communication: An Overview

E. LAMAR ROSS

The study of communication among peoples of diverse linguistic and cultural traditions is not new to anthropologists. It reflects the holistic approach to the study of human cultural traditions that has been characteristic of the discipline since Boas and has made linguistic skills an integral part of an anthropologist's training. Boas emphasized that one could not comprehensively understand the diversity of alien cultural traditions without intimate knowledge of their communication systems. Sapir and Whorf went further by declaring that one's very perception of reality might actually be predetermined by the language one speaks. Modifications over the years—including the "-emic/-etic" dichotomy that arose from the "new ethnography" of the 1960's, and, in addition, the structural approaches of Claude Levi-Strauss and E. R. Leach— have made important contributions to linguistic theory.

The theme of this volume—interethnic communication—presents an interesting challenge to anthropologists: the potential for combining the communication perspective emphasized by Boas with linguistic and communication theories developed not only by anthropologists but also by speech specialists, sociologists, social psychologists, and others interested in the field of interethnic communication.

This volume grew out of the recognition of several facts: (a) Although anthropologists have consistently utilized an operational understanding of interethnic communication in their fieldwork, there were few systematic studies of the process of communication itself.[1] (b) Many of the studies which were available dealing specifically with the theoretical and pragmatic aspects of interethnic communication were works not of anthropologists but instead of social psychologists or specialists in speech communication.[2] (c) Although anthropological concepts and studies were utilized by many of the writers who dealt with interethnic (intercultural) communication, little effort has been made to systematically coordinate efforts between anthropologists and other social scientists in theoretical and pragmatic studies of the process.[3]

The explicit goals of this volume are modest, yet potentially significant. A primary goal is to expose anthropologists and others to various viewpoints on theory, process, and practice in interethnic communication studies. Contributors include anthropologists, a speech communication specialist, a sociologist, and a community organizer. Second, an attempt has been made to provide case studies in interethnic communication that focus on different levels of sociocultural organization—local, national, and international. Ethnographic examples are from Europe, Africa, Asia, and the United States. A final goal is to stimulate other anthropologists—those not already involved in such studies—to actively pursue research and writings in the area of interethnic communication. This may ultimately be the most significant goal.

Although the contributors have utilized the term *interethnic communication* in a wide variety of ways, they shared common ground; all were responding to an abstract that set the goals of the symposium in the following words:

> While one is within one's own cultural tradition, a person is confident of possessing in the majority of social encounters a repertoire of experiences that will permit that person to interpret both the verbal and nonverbal messages transmitted by the other individual. On the other hand, a person's inability to interpret adequately the messages transmitted from members of other cultural or subcultural groups may create problems ranging from mild personal misunderstandings to global war. This symposium will examine the process and problems of interethnic communication and, to some extent, the prospects for improving interethnic communication.

Some papers, those of Yousef and Gumperz, for instance, deal with interethnic interactions of individuals or small groups. Others—those of Smith, Molina, Guillotte, and French—analyze interethnic communication from the perspective of interactions that, although dealing with individuals, emphasize the group similarities and differences. Lieberson and Fox, Aull, and Cimino concern themselves with criteria that relate to the larger social and political entities of the city, state, and nation whose component populations are linguistically or ethnically diverse. One might say then that the unity of the contributions to this volume lies not in their adherence to a particular theoretical perspective, or even to a certain level of sophistication, but rather in the recognition that interethnic communication is a legitimate area for study affecting the wider context of the study of human social interaction.

A PROBLEM RECOGNIZED:
ONE CANNOT NOT COMMUNICATE

Whether we take the position that culture *is* communication and is manifest in different forms, as does Hall (1959), or view communication simply as a process that permits us to interact with others, we must recognize that communication is indispensable to humans.

We cannot *not* communicate. In personal interactions between individuals or through mass media, communication must and does result. Even saying nothing in the presence of others means something.

> Men must communicate, whether or not they will to communicate. . . .
> The theory of Watzlawick and Beavin's argument that "in the presence of another, all behavior is communication" rests on the assumption that communication is inevitable in social situations because all behavior, not only the use of words, is communication, which is not the same as saying that behavior is *only* communicative. Since there is no such thing as nonbehavior, it is impossible not to communicate. (Prosser 1973a: 1)[4]

The question becomes not *whether* we communicate but *what* we communicate. The significance for interethnic relations of the question "What is communicated?" is one that cannot be neglected, whether the concern is with the theoretical implications or strictly with the pragmatic aspects of interactions of diverse ethnic groups on a daily or occasional basis. *Pragmatic* is used here in two ways. In the theoretical realm, what is communicated falls within the pragmatic dimension of human communication,[5] i.e., how verbal and nonverbal signs are related to people and how people react to those signs. Those concerned with daily interactions and the implications for interethnic relations are also interested in the pragmatic, but as it relates to application, not to theoretical concerns.

MANIFESTATION OF A PROBLEM: NONCOMMUNICATION OR MISCOMMUNICATION

How frequently do we fail to convey the intended meaning when we interact with another individual? How frequently do differing linguistic, nonlinguistic, and contextual signals interfere with the message we are attempting to convey? If we take a processual view of communication, we soon realize that the signals one individual sends must pass through a culturally conditioned and constructed barrier before they get to the other individual. Individuals from the same cultural and ethnic background have the least trouble interpreting the signals.[6] The greater the cultural and ethnic differences the more likely it is the message will be misinterpreted, resulting in noncommunication of the intended messages.[7]

At least three results may be encountered: (*a*) some signals will be received as intended (i.e., there is a common base of understanding with little interference); (*b*) some signals are not received because of inter-

vening variables; and (*c*) a different message from that which is sent will
be received (i.e., messages are received but are filtered by intervening
variables). Each of these results is to some extent occurring in all communicative interactions.

Specific examples of such results may be humorous or serious. Chagnon, in his latest edition of *Yanomamo: The Fierce People* (1977), adds
a section dealing with recent acculturative changes and particularly the
impact of missionaries and tourists. He tells of one tourist who awoke
one morning at the mission station, stepped out of the door, and noticed
a Yanomamo rushing off into the woods with his bow and arrow.

> The Western visitor was favorably impressed with the Yanomamo man's
> decorum and politeness, for as the man passed by, he smiled at the visitor
> and said cheerfully: "Ya shii!" The visitor, reciprocally, returned the
> greeting, whereupon the Yanomamo again smiled and said: "Habo. Ya
> barowo." When he reported his exchange of social amenities to the mis-
> sionary, he was a bit distraught at the translation: "I'm on my way to
> defecate." Response: "I have to defecate (also)." Reply: "Come along,
> then; I'll lead the way." (1977 : 161)

Each participant in the conversational interchange had good intentions. The Westerner, of course, was not familiar with the linguistic and
nonlinguistic conventions of the Yanomamo man. He wrongly assumed
that the words were a greeting. The smile accompanying the words likely
added to this misperception of the true meaning. In both cases a message
was being received in a way completely different from that intended by
the participants in the transaction. Each ended the "conversation" be-
lieving that the message had been received, a common mistake in interethnic interactions.

Another incident recounted by Chagnon is no less amusing. In this
instance, the verbal interchange occurred between Chagnon, who speaks
the Yanomamo's language, and a Yanomamo man who was first encountering the industrial world.

After a particularly uncomfortable plane ride through a storm, they
arrived at their destination. Chagnon told his friend to go get in a nearby
car while the bags were being gathered together. In Chagnon's words:

> When I stepped out of the plane, he was standing by the car, examining
> it carefully, glancing periodically at me, then at the car. "Get into it!" I
> shouted. "I'll be right there!" I watched him walk slowly around the car,
> scratch his head, and look up at me with a puzzled expression. "Don't be
> afraid!" I shouted as I walked toward him. "Get in it!" He adjusted the
> tobacco in his mouth, took a half-step toward the car, and dived through
> the open window on the passenger's side, his feet and legs hanging curi-
> ously out of the gaping hole in the side! I had forgotten to tell him about
> doors, and realized how much I had taken things for granted, and how

incredibly bizarre much of our culture would be to the Yanomamo.
(1977 : 143)

These examples, although not uncommon, are of course extreme
when viewed from the perspective of most of our interactions with other
ethnic groups. We are more likely to find ourselves in the situation of
only partially receiving the intended signals, thinking that all parties to
the interaction are in agreement on what has been communicated, even
if not in agreement on the viewpoints expressed. This is the type of situation reported on by Yousef in this volume.

THEORETICAL APPROACHES
TO UNDERSTANDING THE PROBLEM

The major problem in interethnic communication studies is to define
the focus. Although there have been numerous attempts to make fine
distinctions between terms such as *international communication, intercultural communication*, and *interethnic communication* (e.g., see Rich
1974 : 13), ultimately the criteria seem to condense to ones of cultural
differences and identity. One might say, since there are cultural differences implied when we say *interethnic communication*, that the term is
subsumed under the rubric of *intercultural communication*. Without
getting into the controversy of what constitutes ethnic affiliation in our
discussion, we might propose the following as an adequate definition:
"Interethnic communication is communication under conditions of ethnic
differences."[8] This allows for the whole range of studies that are now
considered under the rubric of interethnic communication.
     We can of course specify various approaches to the study of inter-
ethnic communication. These can be placed in three categories: (*a*) approaches to the group; (*b*) approaches to the individual; (*c*) processual
or interaction approaches, each having numerous subvariations and, in
many cases, components that overlap with those of another approach.
All are subsumed under the pragmatic dimension[9] of human communication, and each has its respective emphasis for bettering interethnic
communication.
     Studies in the first category, group approaches, emphasize the defini-
tion of ethnic boundaries and examine the cultural factors in ethnic
identity which affect communication between or among such groups.
One of the foremost works in this area is Fredrik Barth's *Ethnic Groups
and Boundaries* (1969), in which he and other contributors stress the
social organization of cultural differences. In his introduction to the

volume he points out several aspects of ethnic affiliation that are extremely important to the study of interethnic communication.

> The identification of another person as a fellow member of an ethnic group implies a sharing of criteria for evaluation and judgment. It thus entails the assumption that the two are fundamentally "playing the same game.". . . On the other hand, a dichotomization of others as strangers, as members of another ethnic group, implies a recognition of limitations on shared understandings. (1969 : 15)

> The constraints on a person's behavior which spring from his ethnic identity thus tend to be absolute and, in complex poly-ethnic societies, quite comprehensive; and the component moral and social conventions are made further resistant to change by being joined in stereotyped clusters as characteristics of one single identity. (1969 : 17)

Ultimately, with this approach, it becomes a question of "we" versus "they." "Identity," as defined both by self and by others, becomes a major component of any analysis of the mechanics of communication between members of two or more ethnic groups. When one keeps this in mind, prediction of the type of interactions which may occur between members of distinct groups becomes more precise. It is particularly important from the individual's point of view, since when one considers oneself a member of a specific group—even when an outsider might not know the affiliation—one is accepting the liabilities of any negative attitudes others may hold.

Although the group approach gives us a perspective from which to view interaction and communication, it leaves a number of gaps that need to be filled. There appears never to be a direct correlation between self-identification and identification by others in either group membership or language affiliation. Representative illustrations can be given from Chagnon (1977) and Gumperz (1971). Chagnon points out that a common term for neighboring villages of Yanomamo is *Waika*, derived from a verb meaning to "kill an animal (or man) that is already dying from a wound" (1977 : 38). Yet when one asks a member of the next village if he is a *waika*, he always responds in the negative by saying that he is a *yanomamo* and that the *Waika* live in the next village. Gumperz gives us a similar illustration from India concerning the naming of linguistic dialects. The isolated villagers very frequently are unaware of a name for their own dialect but can give a name to neighboring dialects, frequently an uncomplimentary one.

> For instance, there is a well-known form of speech in the south of the Punjab called "Jangali," from its being spoken in the "Jungle," or unirrigated country bordering on Bikaner. But "Jangali," also means "boorish" and local inquiries failed to find a single person who admitted that he spoke that language. "O yes, we know Jangali very well,—you will find

it a little further on,—not here." You go a little further on and get the same reply, and pursue your will-o'-the-wisp till he lands you in the Rajputana desert, where there is no one to speak any language at all. (1971:3)

Concentration on these verbal and nonverbal differences tends to accentuate the differences between individuals and groups rather than the similarities. Common bonds of humanness are obscured by the diversity of norms and values of different cultural traditions. In many areas of the world, this has a correlation with linguistic nationalism movements[10] that have effectively precluded any real communication.

Works that are based on this approach and that emphasize improving interethnic communication concentrate on differences rather than similarities. One who is using this approach must be prepared to recognize the differences that do exist and be willing to utilize that knowledge to improve subsequent interactions with members of other groups. Numerous students of intercultural and interethnic communication utilize this emphasis in at least part of their work (e.g., Fieg and Blair 1975; Condon and Yousef 1975; Harms 1973; Rich 1974; and A. L. Smith 1973).

The second category, individual approaches, concentrates more on the specific linguistic differences between members of ethnic groups and how this affects their personal, individual interaction and communication. The concept of individual encoding and decoding and the idea of interference are communication concepts one might find prevalent in a discussion among those using this approach.

In literature dealing with the linguistic differences within the United States that affect interethnic communication, a frequent example is the difference between Black English and that of most White Americans. This includes not only differences in meanings of certain words held by the two groups (Rich 1974:128), but it also includes an ethnically based speech that has phonological contrasts, loss of suffixes, and other grammatically diverse elements when compared with the standard American form (Burling 1970:117–133).

Gumperz points out in this volume that the differing use of the same linguistic elements by two ethnic groups—even when the numerically subordinate group members speak the majority language—may lead to misunderstanding. This might be due to differences in intonation, in points at which longer utterances are broken into segments, in uses of pronouns, or even in uses of interjections. Shared historical experiences aid members of the same group in understanding the differences in context and content, whereas members of other ethnic groups interpret the linguistic cues in terms of their own cultural experiences.

In some extreme cases, generally politically related, the reverse may be true, that is, linguistic differences may tend to unite a group. One such case can be cited from the south India state of Tamilnad. The Tamil language is noted for its diglossia, "where the literary language preserves archaic features of morphology and phonology, and the spoken language reflects newer developments. So different are the two dialects of Tamil that illiterates can understand only a fraction of the spoken form of the literary language . . . (Schiffman 1973 : 129). It is said that no other spoken language has a written form so different from the spoken.

It would appear that this would in all cases hinder communication if the written form (Pandit Tamil) were verbalized in a communicative context. The DMK Tamil (the Tamil of the Dravidian nationalist political party) is an "alliterative Pandit Tamil" and is not understood by the illiterate Tamil speakers or, for that matter, by most educated Tamil speakers. In spite of the restricted audience that understands it, the alliterative Pandit Tamil has been a unifying force since its significance lies in its context rather than in its content. Its unifying feature lies in its reference to a past that is a revered part of Tamil tradition and that contrasts with the attempts of the national government to impose Hindi as a national language, a non-Dravidian linguistic "upstart" of more recent origin.

For the person relying on an individual approach to the study of interethnic communication, communication between ethnic groups would likely be facilitated by stressing the need for preparing communicators to adapt linguistically. Lieberson presents us in this volume with an analytical tool for describing communication potential within and between groups. One of his assumptions is that increased bilingual capacity increases proportionately the potential for improving interethnic communication, or at least increases communicative possibilities. It is well established that knowledge of another group's language is not a sufficient condition for bettering intergroup relations (e.g., see Gorden 1974). This knowledge is, however, in most cases a necessary condition if one wishes to have positive, long-lasting communicative interaction.

Studies in the third category, processual or interaction approaches, derive primarily from models developed by mathematicians. These models are concerned with the transmission of messages and are the simplest to illustrate diagramatically. Some of the specific labels used for them are (*a*) action performance models, (*b*) interaction models, and (*c*) transactional models.[11] These have in common an emphasis on the presence of a sender, a message, and a receiver. They vary primarily in the type process emphasized.

As Smith pointed out in his *Communication and Culture* (1966), communication models by mathematicians concentrate on syntactics, leaving the study of semantics and pragmatics to social psychologists and linguistic anthropologists. Semantics and pragmatics cannot be neglected when one is dealing with a human population. Such terms as *noise, redundancy,* and *feedback* have little meaning in the abstract when referring to interethnic communication. They are in fact created by cultural differences. They may in fact interfere with the process, resulting in any one of the three message states mentioned earlier in the paper, that is, the message may be received as intended, in a modified form, or not at all.

In fact, noise and other elements of a processual model may purposefully be introduced into an interethnic communicative situation to better one's position in the process. Guillotte, in this volume, refers to such a case among several groups resident in Tanzania. In one instance, the Barabaig are viewed by the researcher as deliberately inserting noise into the governmental system. Members of the group alleging that they could not speak Swahili, the governmental language, in order to put themselves in a better position when they had found themselves in a precarious political situation. In another instance in which it was to their advantage to use Swahili, they inexplicably had learned to argue their own case in the language.

Ultimately, in order to effect social change, proponents following this approach must promote an awareness of the processes involved in daily communicative exchanges and must design means of improving interethnic communication that rely on different processual criteria.

Finally, a few words need to be said concerning the role of the anthropologist in interethnic communication studies. As the variety of papers in this volume illustrates, numerous anthropologists are concerned, both theoretically and pragmatically, with the question of interethnic communication. Each one has approached the problem from his or her own perspective and each has been motivated by a different goal. Each one is contributing something of value, particularly in encouraging others to pursue similar lines of research. Each delineates the problem for research within the boundaries of his or her own theoretical interest.

We should not forget, in addition, that much of the data resulting from anthropological research is being utilized constantly by those who view the knowledge we have presented only as means to an end, that is, as a pragmatic tool for use in practical situations. Anthropologists are in a position to use their theory, their pragmatic intercultural experiences, and the resultant body of knowledge to provide a perspective that can significantly influence the future direction not only of interethnic communication studies but also the use of those studies to better human relations.

This volume is designed as a sounding board for current ideas in anthropological research relating to interethnic communication, but it is more than that. It is an attempt to encourage more cooperation between the diverse elements of the academic community who have a common interest in interethnic communication and to provide a beginning for such interaction. The ultimate outcome lies in the hands of those who may be encouraged by this volume to do further research, attempting to test and expand present theories of interethnic communication.

NOTES

1. There are at least two commonly cited exceptions: Gumperz and Hymes's *Directions in Sociolinguistics: The Ethnography of Communication* (1972) and Alfred G. Smith's *Communication and Culture* (1966).

2. For a discussion of those available up to 1973 see Prosser, *Major Books on Intercultural Communication* (1973b).

3. From the words of some who work daily with the problems in communication of members of other cultures who are trying to adapt to our culture, we learn how others view us. "Many excellent anthropological works provide an insight into the patterns of culture in other societies, but relatively few seem to take a directly contrastive approach to cultural differences, that is to analyze a given aspect of one culture in relation to another. Yet it was exactly this comparative approach that we needed if we were to set our discussions of cultural differences in a context that would be comprehensible to such a diverse group" (Fieg and Blair 1975 : 4).

4. Although a common view among communication theorists, this statement is by no means completely representative. Hymes (1973 : 50) sees it in a different light. "To define communication as the triggering of a response (as Hockett [1958 : 573] has done and Kluckhohn [1961 : 895] has accepted), is to make the term so nearly equivalent to behavior and interaction in general as to lose its specific value as a scientific and moral conception." In my opinion, Hymes's point is operationally valuable, even more in the study of interethnic communication than in the study of intracultural communication.

5. Alfred G. Smith (1966) emphasizes that there are three major dimensions of human communication: (a) syntactics: how signs are related to one another; (b) semantics: how signs are related to things; (c) pragmatics: how signs are related to people or how people react to those signs. We are most concerned in this volume with pragmatics.

6. This does not imply that all communication will be positive or that all individuals within the group easily communicate their intended messages. There is ample evidence that this is not always true.

7. Notice that the emphasis is on the "intended message," since, as we have already stated, one cannot not communicate.

8. This is a paraphrase of Stewart's (1973 : 13) definition of intercultural communication: "communication under conditions of cultural differences."

9. See Alfred G. Smith (1966) and n. 5 above.

10. Two of the most frequently mentioned examples are the French Canadians in Quebec and the Hindi-Urdu conflict in Kashmir. Many former colonies of European nations had to choose official languages that did not represent all segments of the population, e.g., Hindi in India and Swahili in Tanzania. This question is one aspect of ongoing studies by Fox, Aull, and Cimino, represented in this volume.

11. See Stewart (1973 : 8–16) for one person's viewpoint of the differences in these models and for more bibliography.

REFERENCES

Barth, Fredrik, 1969. *Ethnic Groups and Boundaries: The Social Organization of Cultural Difference* (Boston: Little, Brown).

Burling, Robbins, 1970. *Man's Many Voices: Language in its Cultural Context* (New York: Holt, Rinehart, and Winston).

Chagnon, Napoleon A., 1977. *Yanomamo: The Fierce People*, 2nd ed. (New York: Holt, Rinehart, and Winston).

Condon, John C., and Fathi Yousef, 1975. *An Introduction to Intercultural Communication* (New York: Bobbs-Merrill).

Fieg, John P., and John G. Blair, 1975. *There Is a Difference: 12 Intercultural Perspectives* (Washington, D.C.: Meridian House International).

Gorden, Raymond L., 1974. *Living in Latin America: A Case Study in Cross-Cultural Communication* (Skokie, Ill.: National Textbook).

Gumperz, John J., 1971. Some Remarks on Regional and Social Language Differences in India. In *Language in Social Groups: Essays by John J. Gumperz*, Anwar S. Dil, ed. (Palo Alto, Cal.: Stanford University Press).

Gumperz, John J., and Dell Hymes, eds., 1972. *Directions in Sociolinguistics: The Ethnography of Communication* (New York: Holt, Rinehart and Winston).

Hall, Edward, 1959. *The Silent Language* (New York: Doubleday).

Harms, L. S., 1973. *Intercultural Communication* (New York: Harper and Row).

Hockett, Charles F., 1958. *A Course in Modern Linguistics* (New York: Macmillan).

Hymes, Dell, 1973. Toward Ethnographies of Communication. In *Intercommunication Among Nations and Peoples*, Michael H. Prosser, ed. (New York: Harper and Row).

Kluckhohn, Clyde, 1961. Notes on Some Anthropological Aspects of Communication. *American Anthropologist* 63 : 895–910.

Prosser, Michael H., 1973a. *Intercommunication Among Nations and Peoples* (New York: Harper and Row).

———, 1973b. *Major Books on Intercultural Communication* (Pittsburgh, Pa.: Intercultural Communications Network).

Rich, Andrea, 1974. *Interracial Communication* (New York: Harper and Row).

Schiffman, Harold, 1973. Language, Linguistics, and Politics in Tamilnad.

In *Studies in the Language and Culture of South Asia,* Edwin Gerow and Margery D. Lang, eds. (Seattle: University of Washington Press).

Smith, A. G., 1966. *Communication and Culture: Readings in the Codes of Human Interaction* (New York: Holt, Rinehart and Winston).

Smith, Arthur L., 1973. *Transracial Communication* (Englewood Cliffs, N.J.: Prentice-Hall).

Stewart, John, 1973. *Bridges Not Walls: A Book About Interpersonal Communication* (Menlo Park, Cal.: Addison-Wesley).

The Conversational Analysis of Interethnic Communication

JOHN J. GUMPERZ

Communication is power in modern postindustrial society.[1] Control over one's life in all arenas depends on the ability to communicate effectively; private life increasingly involves dealings with public agencies, and effectiveness in business, employment, and public administration is a function of the ability to justify opinions and settle differences. Human relations everywhere entail enlisting support and approval, but nowadays people must deal with others whose social and communicative backgrounds differ significantly from theirs and who consequently do not share their basic assumptions. While these communicative conditions apply throughout modern society, they place a special burden on urban ethnic minorities from economically poor regions who, during the last decade, have come to occupy an important place in the industrial labor force.

In this chapter I will discuss the role of communication in interethnic relations. I will attempt to show that communication difficulties that arise in certain key situations—for instance, committee meetings, job interviews, and industrial disputes where participants' abilities and attitudes are evaluated—are due to differences in the perception and interpretation of conventional verbal and nonverbal signals. These signals are habitually produced and interpreted, yet failure to understand how they operate contributes to the atmosphere of uncertainty and unpredictability, aggravates intergroup tension, and leads to personal frustration and powerlessness.

Interethnic relations in advanced industrial societies offer a challenge to our most commonly held assumptions about culture and communication. Existing social theory tends to characterize contact between cultures in terms of one or the other of two conceptual frameworks: the plural society model or the notion of assimilation in the urban melting pot.

The term *plural society* refers to large population aggregates such as are found in ex-colonial agricultural regions or trading centers where several distinct ethnic groups coexist within a single geographical space and live under the same governmental and economic system. Generally, each one of these ethnic groups occupies its own neighborhood and maintains its own informal local institutions and religious organizations. Although an individual in such a situation regularly interacts with members of other ethnic groups, he or she nevertheless carries on daily affairs surrounded by kin and friends. The person's closest and most meaningful contacts take place within in-group networks, where the communicative etiquette is different from that of other local groups and the medium of interaction is either the language of the original home- land or a pidgin, creole, or ethnic dialect. Under these circumstances, relations with outsiders tend to be confined to instrumental or goal- oriented interactions, such as business or market dealings—highly for- malized or ritualized exchanges or casual encounters where only limited amounts of information are conveyed. When contact with officialdom or with the dominant regional elites is necessary, it is mediated either by locals who have shown special ability for intergroup communication or members of the elite experienced in such matters.

Acculturation, on the other hand, occurs when individuals or small family groups enter a new region that is otherwise generally homo- geneous or at least dominated by a homogeneous culture; over time, they become gradually absorbed into the dominant group, giving up their own values, traditions, and language to take on those prevalent in their new environment.

Neither one of the above models accounts for the conditions we en- counter in Europe and the United States, where a significant part of the industrial labor force is made up of minority group members from agricultural or economically underdeveloped regions. At first glance, it might seem that these groups live under conditions similar to those found in plural societies. In most instances their home backgrounds tend to be similar. They move to the urban center in extended family groups; they come from a small set of villages or towns and settle close to each other, forming highly visible subgroupings that make up a large percentage of the populations in a specific industrial center. Once established, they tend to create religious and cultural organizations that mirror those of the homeland, so that much of their informal interaction takes place among others of similar backgrounds. The very nature, however, of the urban environment in which they must function—the increasing bureau- cratization of government agencies that control necessary housing, wel- fare, and health services, as well as the bureaucratization of industrial management at work—impose conditions of intergroup contact with communicative requirements that go beyond the limited kinds of inter-group contact we find in the economically less complex plural societies.

Bureaucratization of public life in the modern welfare state has brought about the elimination of the stratum of informal leaders and intermediaries who formerly played a key role in communication between local people and official organizations. At the same time, as govern-mental agencies arise to control matters of housing, education, health, and welfare, as commercial enterprise becomes subject to licensing, and as conflict resolution becomes a matter of public arbitration rather than private settlement, individuals have become increasingly dependent on their own ability to deal with officialdom. Complex forms must be filled out, and rigidly prescribed but often poorly explained procedures have to be followed. Instead of the former intermediaries who were familiar with the culture and concerns of the local population, there now is a host of poorly paid and often ill-educated, harassed, and overworked public officials who have little understanding of cultural differences but whose job it is to see to the observance of bureaucratic procedures as they allocate services and resources in accordance with criteria that are rarely understood by the supposed beneficiaries.

There is, in addition, increasing government regulation and unioni-zation in industrial establishments where workers are employed, with the result that skills of persuasion or argumentation are needed that are far different from those required in more traditional intergroup situa-tions. In fact, whether an individual is successful in these environments is often more a matter of skill in communicating with native speakers than of technical know-how. It is not enough to be able to do one's job well, to be skillful as a craftsman, technician, or office worker. One has to be able to demonstrate one's abilities to others who judge within the system of cultural values and communicative strategies of the dominant groups and who are unaware of the effects of cultural differences. To the extent that cultural differences persist, there is a real clash between the communicative skills and strategies that are effective within the home and friendship circles and those that are effective in public settings where majority group conventions prevail. Minority group members un-aware of the relevant differences regularly find themselves misunder-stood. They see their intentions misread, find it difficult to predict the reactions of others, and feel an increasing sense of powerlessness to manage their own lives.

Such communication problems have not gone unnoticed in the litera-ture on interethnic relations, but so far differences in values, goals, and attitudes are cited as the major problem. Obviously, these cultural fac-tors play an important role. But the crucial issue is how cultural differences influence interaction and how they affect seemingly straightforward judgments of ability and intent. Furthermore, not all culturally divergent groups have equally severe communication problems, nor do all members of any one group. In the following discussion I attempt to examine the factors that account for these differences in communicative effectiveness. I take examples from my work with Indian and Pakistani workers in London, which is one of a series of comparative studies of interethnic situations in urban England and in the United States.

ASIANS IN LONDON

Immigration from South Asia to England began in the 1950's and reached its peak during the 1960's but has stopped since the early 1970's as a result of economic decline. Indian and Pakistani immigrants to London often come from isolated farm villages; before arriving in Great Britain they had little or no acquaintance with conditions they would face there. By now most of the immigrant workers are fairly well established in a number of industrial suburbs throughout southeast England, the Midlands, and parts of the north of England. There are a number of Hindu and Muslim religious institutions and networks of voluntary organizations patterned on those of the homeland, as well as Indian-owned shops and restaurants, which cement local social cohesion. Industrial wages, although originally very low, are by now comparable with those of English workers in similar categories.

According to traditional acculturation theory, one might assume that as settlement progresses, as the new immigrants gradually become familiar with their environment and with the lifestyle of the majority, and as majority members become accustomed to minority groups, problems of culture contact would decrease. However, this has not been the case. On the contrary, there is evidence to show that in many situations interethnic relations are deteriorating, and communication difficulties are beginning to grow rather than diminish with increased interethnic contact. In many industries where Indian workers have been a regular part of the work force for almost decades, intergroup tension is growing. Other English workmen, union stewards, and foremen, as well as lower-level managers, have come to form fairly rigid stereotypes of Indian workers as clannish and unwilling to make friends or to participate in organized social activities. They resent the use of Hindi, Punjabi, or other non-English languages when others are present. Foremen complain that Indian workers show little interest in improving production, have a high rate of absenteeism, and seem interested only in collecting their paychecks.

The Indians and Pakistanis, in turn, show mounting impatience with the failure of majority group members to understand their needs. They complain of injustice on the part of management and unions in all areas. In particular, many are acutely aware of the discrepancy between what they know is their own considerable technical ability and the judgments others make of their work. Seeing no explanation for this discrepancy, they believe they are victims of racial discrimination. On almost every shop floor one finds cases of individuals who were relatively well educated in India, are technically highly accomplished, and are well respected among their peers but who somehow never gain recognition from supervisors. Unable to perform well on tests or to present their positions convincingly in the presence of foremen or other officials, and ineffective in interview situations, they repeatedly find themselves passed over for promotion, while others advance who in peer opinion are less capable but who somehow seem to be able to catch the eye of the native English speakers.

Since Indians and Pakistanis are not native speakers of English, one might assume that their communication problems are simply due to their lack of knowledge of the language, but the problem is more complex than that. To begin with, English has been an official medium in India and Pakistan for centuries, and many of the immigrants already had at least a reading knowledge of the language. By now, after almost a decade in Britain, almost all of them, with the exception of those who spend all their time within their local neighborhoods, have at least a functional control of English.

For those who need it, language instruction is available, either through local community centers or through the state adult education system. In recent years the Department of Employment has established a National Center for Industrial Language Training, which sets up and coordinates on-site language instruction in industrial establishments where minority workers are employed. The center staff has conducted a number of in-depth studies of industrial communication situations throughout England and has found that difficulties do not necessarily disappear as the workers gain control of basic English grammar and vocabulary. In many cases language teachers are quite satisfied with workers' progress in the classroom, yet on the shop floor, foremen and supervisors find little improvement in their performance. They also found that disputes resulting in communication failures arise not only with speakers who have minimal control of English but just as frequently with those who know

English well. Clearly the problem is not simply knowledge of the language. Nor is the question simply one of foreign accent or second-language interference of the type that has been studied by psycholinguists. Greek and Cypriot immigrants often have accents which, measured in purely linguistic terms, are even more deviant than those of Indians and Pakistanis, but yet they have less difficulty communicating.

Communication difficulties between native English speakers and Indians occur primarily in longer goal-oriented encounters, such as negotiations or discussions, mishaps requiring a participant to justify his actions, promotion interviews, or hearings in local agencies. All these are situations in which talk is the basis for judgments about speakers' abilities and attitudes. The question we want to ask, then, is what it is about talk, apart from grammar, that leads to such judgments. In order to examine this question, my associates and I tape-recorded numerous interactions involving Indian and Pakistani workers in industrial and other settings. In what follows I will analyze several excerpts from these tapes.

The first example comes from a discussion, or rather an argument, between a young female staff member in an industrial language-teaching unit and a middle-aged male Indian worker. The worker was employed in a neighboring factory and was at the time a participant in a class on communication skills. He had heard that applications were available at the center for a new, more advanced course on communication problems being organized at a local community college. Interested in enrolling, he had asked for a copy of the form. When the center staff delayed in giving him an application, he went directly to the community college. When he secured an application from them, he concluded that the center staff had been discriminating against him in not giving him one. He did not accept the explanation that the forms had been held up in the mail. He therefore sought out a center staff member who would be one of several lecturers in the course to protest this perceived discrimination and convince her that they were wrong in thinking he was not qualified to take the course.

In the discussion that ensued, the staff member pointed out that the new course was designed for professionals such as teachers, social workers, and labor relations officers, not for laymen. The Indian worker's argument, which emerged implicitly later in the interaction, was that he would like to become such a professional and should therefore be admitted to the course. This worker, in fact, had graduated from college in India and had come to England some ten years before. He had taken an industrial job expecting to be promoted to professional status in due time. His is a typical case of the sort cited above, characterized by a striking disparity between technical ability and professional success. The discussion between this worker and the staff member was recorded by a second center staff member without the participants' knowledge. When they were apprised of the recording, however, they both agreed to its use. After it was analyzed, both participants listened to the recording and concurred with the main features of our analysis. A transcript of the conversation follows:

TEACHER: Mrs. N. and Mrs. G. thought originally that it was a course to carry on with the twilight course but this is not the case.

WORKER: No. What you you take one thing at a time you . . . take it that whatever they know I get that even mmm for a D. (speaker's name)
5 me and I am student in E. Technical College and Mr. W. knows me. He . . . I asked for him in the same school. He knows my qualifications and what . . . uh whether I am suitable or not.

TEACHER: But this has nothing to do with. . . .

WORKER: But you can't know and can't tell a person just uh to come
10 into this course. If . . . suppose I came to this course from uh. . . . Had you taken this impression that I am not suitable because I took this course.

TEACHER: But it's a question of the job you're doing. The course is for people who. . . . I'll tell you . . . it says on the information it's for youth employment officers. It's for members of the police. It's for ah teachers.
15 It's for people in management positions. Those are the people who are going to be in the course.

WORKER: Yes uh that's uh that's your plan and that ih you make it a . . .

TEACHER: But Mr. Mr. D. it's a training course for people who are
20 going to do those jobs.

WORKER: and and it lasts until you say. I . . . the people who are interested in this ih sort of uh . . . ed-education

TEACHER: Yes. With reference to their work, yes. Yes.

WORKER: Yes.
25 TEACHER: Exactly. With reference to their work.

WORKER: Profe . . . professional people them or all the people who are personally interested.

TEACHER: Why are you so uni-. . . . You've applied. It doesn't matter anymore.
30 WORKER: Yes.

TEACHER: I don't understand . . . why you are so insulted with me.

WORKER: mm I . . . I am not insulting you.

The tape begins in the midst of a heated exchange. Voices are raised; speakers frequently interrupt each other and seem to be paying little attention to what the other has to say. The staff member is clearly annoyed. As the argument develops, she becomes increasingly frustrated by her inability to get through, until she finally breaks out with, "I don't understand why you are so insulted with me." At times the worker appears almost unresponsive; at other times he seems to shout. Moreover, his speech seems halting and lacking in fluency by native English standards. In longer utterances, his meaning is difficult to grasp.

Thus our first impression is that the Indian worker lacks control of English. His pronunciation does indeed show a heavy Indian English accent. However when we examine individual sentences, we find that, aside from the false starts, self corrections, and changes in topic, which are quite common in heated exchanges and can also be found in the staff member's talk, violations of basic grammatical rules characteristic of first-language interference are minor and do not impede comprehension, as for example in the omission of the indefinite article in "I am student . . ." (line 5). The most problematic aspect of the worker's speech is the way phrases are strung together, not their internal grammatical structure.

How do we analyze interactions of this kind? In spite of the recent growth of interest in language variation and bilingualism, there is little sociolinguistic theory that deals with conversational inference in longer verbal exchanges. Most types of sociolinguistic analysis begin with linguistic data based on analyses of single sentences in terms of their referential meaning and correlate these with social data collected according to the usual social science paradigms. When the social appropriateness of certain linguistic forms is studied, measurement has relied on rating scales by which respondents classify verbal data in terms of analytical categories devised by analysts, in interview contexts which are quite different from those of the original interaction (Shuy, Wolfram, and Riley 1968; Labov 1973; Lambert 1973). There is an implicit assumption in such attitude measurements, moreover, that participants share rules of interpretation and that misunderstanding presents no problem.

More relevant for our purposes than previous sociolinguistic studies is the recent work in linguistic pragmatics and philosophy of language that is directly concerned with the processes by which hearers interpret what the speaker intends to achieve with a message (Cole and Morgan 1975). Pragmaticists have shown that interpretation of communicative intent is not predictable on the basis of referential meaning alone. Matters of context, social presuppositions, knowledge of the world, and individual background knowledge all play an important role in interpretation. Yet even though linguistic pragmaticists talk about studying conversations, their formal investigations have been confined to single sentences or very brief exchanges produced by educated speakers in socially homogeneous situations. As in most other types of linguistic inquiry, it is assumed that given a stretch of speech and a rough specification of the context in which it was produced, speaker and hearer can readily agree on what is intended. No attempt has been made to account for situations such as those in interethnic settings where the referential meaning of individual sentences is understood by all concerned, but what differs are interpretations of intent. No one, moreover, has shown how speakers go about integrating their grammatical knowledge with the social presuppositions and contextual information that also enter into the interpretation process.

The pragmaticists' concern with defining meaning in terms of speakers' intent and their recognition that judgments of intent are based on more than surface meaning are fundamental to conversational analysis. Additional conceptual apparatus is needed, however, to account for the issues we have raised.

The theoretical basis for the present study derives from our own previous work on conversation, which concentrates on the analysis of long, complete episodes in which communicative effect can be studied directly by juxtaposing evidence within the interaction itself and data gathered by elicitation procedures. Once the outcome of the episode is known from internal evidence, one can proceed to analyze the verbal strategies by which this outcome was achieved. Internal evidence is obtained through direct examination of the process of interspeaker coordination, that is, of turn-taking or speaker-change strategies, or rhythmic coordination of statements and responses, and of the semantic ties among component messages (Turner 1974; Erickson 1975). External evidence is gathered through questioning strategies in which participants themselves are asked to (*a*) recall what was intended at a particular point in an interaction, and (*b*) pinpoint the perceptions of style and content that led to their interpretation. These questioning procedures are particularly useful in cases where participants differ in their interpretation of the component messages, because it can be shown that such differences are often based on unverbalized, hitherto unrecognized, but nevertheless systematic differences in the perception of linguistic signs (Gumperz 1976). Our example is an instance of an episode just long enough for detailed analysis, although it is in itself part of a longer interaction, which is being analyzed in its entirety (Aulakh and VanValin 1977).

The staff member's final exasperated utterance, "I don't understand . . . why you are so insulted with me," and the worker's reply, "I am not insulting you," show that the episode ends in complete misunderstanding. After preliminary transcription and analysis, we asked both participants to go over the passage and comment on their reactions.

The staff member stated that she felt that the worker's behavior was hostile and inconsistent. On several occasions he first seemed to agree with what she said and then unexpectedly contradicted her. She felt he was questioning her competence and her sincerity. In the end, when she said (lines 28–29), "It doesn't matter anymore," referring to the fact that he did receive an application, the calm tone of his reply, "Yes," implied to her that it had never really mattered to him. She then lost her temper and asked why he was so insulted. As evidence for her negative evaluations, the staff member pointed to the worker's repeated use of interjections such as "No," in line 3, which she understood as indicating agreement with her statement in line 2, "This is not the case," as well as his "Yes" in line 30, which also seemed to indicate agreement, followed by his renewed persistent arguing and occasional shouting, as in "but you can't know!" At another point, when she stated (lines 19–20) that the course was intended as a training course for people who already held certain jobs, he said calmly (line 21), "and it lasts until you say." Here again although his tone of voice suggested agreement, the content implied that he was accusing her of being arbitrary.

The Indian worker, on the other hand, had quite different interpretations. He commented on the staff member's high pitch and tone, which he interpreted as emotional and therefore impolite. He said that she interrupted him and paid no attention to the relevant information he was presenting. When asked what he meant when he said "No" in line 3, he said he did not agree with her and therefore there was no inconsistency with his later remarks. He also said that he was not shouting at any point in the conversation; he was simply trying to recapture the floor when he felt he was being interrupted.

Clearly, the misunderstanding here is not simply based on misreading of sentence content. Some of the differences in interpretation are directly traceable to particular discourse features, or "contextualization cues," as we will call them. To understand how these discourse features operate for members of local Indian English-speaking networks, let us look at a second episode, taken from our recordings of in-group speech where all participants have similar communicative backgrounds.

In this episode an Indian social worker is conducting a discussion with workers from a nearby plant about the problem of securing mortgages. The social worker was born in Malaysia and spent some time in East Africa before going to London. Her native language is Punjabi, but she has lived in London for most of her adult life. When talking to educated speakers of English she has a slight accent but her style is native-like syntactically and in terms of discourse structure. When talking to relatively uneducated members of the local community, as she herself observed, she instinctively adapts her communicative style to that of her audience. The speech represented in the discussion, then, can serve as a good illustration of local Indian English communicative conventions.

The recording begins after the investigator has entered the room, has been introduced, and has received permission to record the class.

TEACHER: (*turning to the class*) Can we go back again on it please. Because uh I don't like to . . . say. Cause before I talk I'd like to hear again. We're talking about uh . . . how to get a mortgage. (turning to investigator): I don't know if . . . you know anything about the English system
5 here.

INVESTIGATOR: I do.

TEACHER (*turning again to the class*): Mortgages. If you have to buy a house, who can get, and who cannot get. What assumptions we made. What if you work. . . . If you don't work can you get a mortgage?
10 STUDENT: No but is it so that if you all . . . even men if you are not married and you are working.

TEACHER: First of all if you're not working there is no chance of getting a mortgage.

STUDENT: No.
15 TEACHER: Unless you have all the money you see but then we are not talking about mortgage. Because mortgage meaning to borrow the money. Where from.

(Student answers smoothly, giving no sign of not understanding)

Judged by the standards of English conversation, the style of this discussion is clearly odd. To begin with, the flow of talk does not strike a native English speaker as smooth. The rhythm seems halting and gives the impression that the speakers lack fluency. Many sentences, clauses, and phrases, furthermore, seem incomplete, and logical connections between contiguous statements are difficult for us to discern. In the following stretch of speech, for example, there is nothing in the first sentence to prepare the hearer for the question which follows it: "Because mortgages meaning to borrow the money. Where from." As a result, a native English speaker has difficulty determining the object to which the question refers. Nevertheless, the participants in the discussion seem to have no trouble understanding each other. The students show no hesitation in answering the social worker. The answers themselves, however, also seem odd to native English speakers. When the social worker, for example, says, "There is no chance of getting a mortgage," the student answers, "No," apparently denying what she has said. Yet she gives no sign that anything is wrong and goes on with her argument.

The features that make the discussion seem odd are similar to those that appeared in the Indian worker's speech in our first example, yet here they create no problem. We hypothesize therefore that they reflect a system of contextualization conventions that is shared by members of local Indian English-speaking networks.

In what follows we will try to describe three elements of that system: (*a*) paralinguistic and prosodic cues, (*b*) deictic pronouns (pronouns that are interpretable only by reference to preceding utterances), and (*c*) interjections such as *yes* and *no* by which listeners signal their reactions to what has been said.

Paralinguistic and prosodic cues are features such as intonation, stress, rhythm, and sentence speed, which characterize all spoken utterances. The phonetic aspects of these features have been investigated in considerable detail in recent years, and it has furthermore been shown that they play an important role in signaling attitudes (Crystal 1975). But if we look at their functioning in verbal interactions we find that they are also crucial to the strategies that participants use in signaling degrees of inter-speaker cooperation and channeling and controlling the flow of conversation. To understand how this works, let us look more closely at some of these features and how they operate in our examples.

Prosody involves three distinct signaling mechanisms: (*a*) tone grouping, (*b*) tonic or nucleus placement, and (*c*) tune. Tone grouping is the use of intonation contours along with pauses to subdivide messages into smaller chunks. The chunks created in this way must of course bear some relation to the syntax of the utterance, but there are always many more possible syntactic boundaries than are actually used in the tone grouping of particular utterances. A speaker, therefore, can choose to combine certain message parts into a single tone group and thereby separate it from the rest of the utterance for emphasis or other semantic purpose. Nucleus placement refers to the positioning of the major-stressed syllable within a tone group. This stressed syllable is the site of the change in pitch which marks the intonational contour. In English, nucleus placement is an important way of marking new information in contrast with that part of the message which is regarded as known or given (Chafe 1974). Tune refers to the direction of change of the nuclear tone pattern. In English this can be a fall (as in the previous example), or a rise, or a combination of rise-fall or fall-rise. It is common to associate rising tunes with questions and falling tunes with statements, but in discourse, in contrast to the simple sentences which are ordinarily used in phonetic studies of prosody, the functions are much more complex. Thus a rise may be used to signal that an utterance is incomplete, that is, that more is coming, or that what is being said is to be interpreted with reference to what is to follow. A fall in tune indicates that a message is complete, or independent of what follows, and perhaps characterizes the statement as definite or assertive.

Distinct from the prosodic cues of nucleus placement and tune are paralinguistic features of pitch register, loudness, and rhythm, which apply to entire tone groups or sets of tone groups rather than parts thereof. It is important to distinguish between, on the one hand, the normal discourse function of prosodic and paralinguistic cues as devices necessary in the production of conversation, and on the other their expressive use in the process of conversational inference. In their discourse function, these cues are necessary to maintain cohesion in any speech chain. The particular ways in which they are used, however, and the relative reliance on one of the several mechanisms we have mentioned rather than another, is a function of culturally determined communicative conventions.

Another matter subject to cultural variation is the mapping of these suprasegmental features onto the words spoken. Speakers' knowledge of both the selection of prosodic and paralinguistic devices and their relation to sentence structure and content takes the form of cooccurrence expectations learned by interactive experience. These cooccurrence expectations are not only culturally specific but are closely related to communicative background and the network of social relationships that determine this background (Gumperz 1976).

The second example illustrates how these culturally determined features are realized in the conversation of the Indian speakers in our examples. After examining these, I will then return to the interethnic conversation in which the breakdown occurred, to show how these features affected the interpretation process. I will concentrate on the function of prosodic and paralinguistic cues and only briefly refer to the other cues that have been mentioned, deictic pronouns and interjections.

The first sentence in example two was spoken as follows:

⌐Can we go bạck / again on it plęạse. // [2]

This sentence is split into two tone groups, and the boundary between them divides what sounds to native speakers of English as a single verb phrase, *go back again*. Such a tone group boundary conflicts with native English cooccurrence expectations. (A possible tone group boundary for a native English speaker might be before *please*). The first tone group has slightly higher pitch register and loudness than the second. This pattern of contrasting pitch registers within a sentence also sounds odd to a native English speaker. In native English, high pitch generally indicates the introduction of a new topic, or some sort of emphasis, and extends over the entire message unit. Moreover, although I have marked nucleus placement, nuclear stress is more difficult to identify with a pitch extractor in Indian English than it is in equivalent samples of native London speech. Preliminary investigation indicates some of the discourse functions of nucleus placement in native English are assumed in Indian English by pitch register (Gumperz, Agrawal and Aulakh 1977).

These signaling patterns occur throughout example two as well as in other tape recordings of in-group speech we have collected. We can now apply this knowledge to the intergroup situation. Let us look, for example, at the sentence that was already identified as odd in our earlier discussion:

> Because mortgage meaning / to borrow the money / / whère from / /

The tone group boundaries again are odd from the point of view of native English syntax. Our English conventions would lead us to expect the first boundary after *mortgage* rather than after *meaning*. Furthermore, if the tone boundary were placed after *mortgage*, that word would have to carry low rising tune, in order to indicate that the second phrase is semantically connected to the first one. In this example it carries falling tune, which makes it difficult for native English speakers to grasp the connection between the two parts of the utterance. Note also the high falling tune of the question "Where from." In other words, the pitch goes up on *where* and down on *from*. An English speaker, if she used the same phrase, would have to do the reverse, placing rising tune on *from*.

Apart from prosody and paralinguistics, there are also several oddities in the use of interjections and of deictic pronouns (that is, pronouns that can only be interpreted by reference to some other part of the conversation or extralinguistic context). The role of such mechanisms in signaling discourse cohesion is similar to that of the other cues we have been discussing. In the first sentence, "Can we go back / again on it please /," a native speaker of English has difficulty finding a referent for *it*. From other data as well as this, it seems that in Indian English the deictic pronoun *it* can refer to the extralinguistic context rather than to any specific preceding utterance much more freely than it can in English. A native English speaker would more likely say, "Let's go back again please."

Similarly, the Indian English speaker may include a deictic pronoun where a native English speaker would not expect it. In the following sentences, which were spoken later in the mortgage discussion, a pronoun seems lacking:

> The banks don't lend you for twenty-five or thirty years. The banks don't lend you for that long.

With respect to interjections such as *yes* and *no*, in British English (as in American English) these responses indicate either agreement or disagreement with someone else's preceding statement, although *yes* can sometimes serve merely as a discourse filler. In our Indian English conversations, both *yes* and *no* are simply a way of indicating "I have heard you." The tendency is to acknowledge a preceding negative statement with a *no*, and a preceding affirmative statement with a *yes*, although this is not strictly adhered to.

In summary, then, although there is no space to go into detail about these matters here, there is ample evidence to show that contextualization cues in Indian English are systematic and differ significantly from those in British English. In order to corroborate our hypothesis about the origin of the Indian English system, we translated some of our Indian English transcripts into informal colloquial Punjabi, the native language of several of the discourse participants in our data. The translation was made in such a way as to preserve the rhythmic and prosodic features of the Indian English original. Speakers of Punjabi who listened to the tape-recorded translation readily characterized the conversation as quite normal, fluent talk.

Given our understanding of the importance of contextualization cues in conversational inference and our demonstration of the significant differences in the function of these cues in Indian English and British English, we hypothesize that the conflicting evaluations of the two participants in our first examples are directly due to their use of differing systems and their lack of awareness of this fact. A few illustrations will provide additional examples of how this can be seen in the conversation between the British staff member and the Indian worker. I will return to some of the evaluative comments made by the staff member to demonstrate how they relate to contextualization conventions.

I have already mentioned the staff member's reference to what seemed inconsistent to her in the worker's signaling of agreement by his use of interjections and then disagreeing with her. Now that we know the interjections *yes* and *no* do not necessarily indicate agreement or disagreement, we can explain the discrepancy. The allegation that the Indian worker was shouting can be explained if we note that the Indian worker uses the paralinguistic features of increased loudness and pitch register to claim the floor when he has been interrupted. This is another paralinguistic discourse function such as the ones we have seen (Agrawal 1976). A native English speaker will try to regain the floor by more direct verbal means, such as "I didn't finish."

It can furthermore be seen that the impression of lack of fluency is due to the use of unexpected tone grouping and nucleus placement. The worker's first long statement was spoken as follows:

No // what you . . . / you take one thing / at a time // you . . . take it
// that whatever they know // I get that / even mmm for a Ḍ. [speaker's

name] // me // and I am student in E. Technical College // and Mr. W. knows me // he . . . I asked for him / in the same school // he knows my qualifications / and what . . . // uh whether I am suitable or not //

The initial difficulty here is with the "No," which was uttered with a low fall. This "No" follows the very emphatic "This is not the case," spoken by the staff member. The staff member interprets this as an indication of acceptance of what she said because of the low falling tune. For her to understand it as a disagreement, the "No" would have had to have a high falling tune.

Furthermore, when he says

Whatever they know // I get that //

the speaker means to draw a parallel between what they, the students who will take the course, know and what he knows. It is true that a modal *can* or *could* in *I could get that* would make the meaning clearer, but the sentence could have been understood as it is if nucleus placement had signaled the contrast between the two phrases by highlighting the relevant words *they* and *I* through nucleus placement and tune. Instead, this speaker marks this contrast by raising pitch register and loudness on the entire first tone group and lowering them on the entire second tone group. The first tone group, moreover, ends with a low fall on *know*, so that a native English speaker does not look for a semantic connection with the following phrase.

Finally, after saying "I get that," the worker continues with the qualifying phrase, "even for a D. [his name] / me //" and then adds, "and I am student in E. [college name] Technical College //." In these latter two phrases the pitch is low and loudness decreases progressively. Yet, the last phrase presents new and crucial information. It informs the staff member for the first time that in addition to taking courses at the center, he is also registered at the community college where the course in which he wants to enroll is to be taught. It emerged in our subsequent discussion that the staff member completely missed this point. Apparently she did not expect new and important information to be communicated by a shift from high to low pitch and in a low voice. Her cooccurrence expectations led her to listen carefully to the preceding phrase, "me," whose content seemed unimportant and redundant. The Indian worker, then, was correct in accusing her of not listening to the relevant information, but she had of course not done so intentionally.

This is just a brief indication of the ways in which differences in contextualization conventions can lead to negative evaluations in encounters that are very important to individuals' social or occupational success.

In order to learn to communicate with each other, both the staff member and the worker need to engage in interactions of this sort and then to examine the interactions critically and discuss what led to their evaluations. But this sort of metacommunication rarely happens. All too often, situations like this contribute to a vicious circle in which participants evade direct confrontation, and the consequent negative experiences lead them to avoid further involvement with those who employ similar verbal strategies.

The tragic aspect of this pattern is that while the cause of communication breakdown is mutual—that is, neither participant knows enough about the strategies employed by the other to maintain conversation and to reliably evaluate the attitudes and abilities of the other—it is the minority group member who usually suffers. Because of the elements of power and economic inequality that prevail in minority-majority contact, it is generally the minority group member who is judged and evaluated and therefore has most to lose if communication breaks down in such gatekeeping situations.

CONCLUSION

We have argued that communication difficulties arise as a result of habitual verbal and nonverbal strategies that subconsciously affect judgments of attitudes and abilities. These contextualization phenomena tend to go unnoticed in everyday situations, although their effect is constantly felt. They are learned in the course of previous interactive experience. To the extent that such interactive experience is a function of home background, and insofar as home background relates to ethnicity, knowledge of such rhetorical conventions is ethnically determined. This is particularly true for individuals who, like the Indian and Pakistani workers we have studied, live and interact largely within in-group networks. They are surrounded by peers of similar backgrounds on whom they rely for emotional and economic support. The strategies of persuasion and argumentation that fail to work in encounters with majority group members are the very strategies that serve to build and reinforce these networks among those who share them.

Given the repeated failure of these strategies, one might of course ask why speakers do not learn to adapt them in the same way that they acquire grammar. For one thing, difficulties are not generally recognized as communication breakdowns. Judgments, rather, are made on the mistaken assumption that intent is understood. In part of the preceding argument not transcribed here, the staff member accuses the worker of being "silly" (and, incidentally, using a term which to Indians is a highly insulting way of addressing an older person). At the same time the worker insists that the teacher is purposely withholding information from him, even though she herself is convinced she is doing all she can to accommodate him.

A further problem is that contextualization conventions are context bound and therefore not readily amenable to classroom teaching. They are best learned through practice in actual interaction where errors can be good-naturedly corrected, such as peer or family relations. Moreover, when people we know well seem to evidence strange verbal behavior, we operate on the assumption that they are reasonable people of good will. Therefore we may scrutinize our own understanding of what is happening rather than laying blame on them. Interethnic situations, however, are conducted within a context of mutual suspicion, or at least without the predisposition to assume cooperation on the part of the other. Finally, the very situations in which minority and majority groups most often interact are such that the power relationships prevent misunderstandings from being recognized and therefore preclude the learning of new strategies.

Miscommunication is a two-way matter. Both participants fail to understand and be understood because their cultural presuppositions do not match. In interethnic situations of the kind we have described, however, only the majority group members have the ability to justify their interpretations before other authorities who share their system. Minority group members, on the other hand, when they seek to justify themselves, are subject to the same problems of misinterpretation that led to their frustration in the first place. This is the dilemma of interethnic communication.

NOTES

1. Research for this paper was supported by NIMH grant MH26831-03. I am grateful to E. Laird and H. Doodi for cooperation in fieldwork and analysis. Gurinder Aulakh and Robert Van Valin assisted in the data analysis. Deborah Tannen helped with the preparation and organization of the manuscript. I am grateful to all of them for many helpful suggestions.
2. A single clash indicates a minor tone group boundary. A double slash indicates a major tone group boundary. The diacritic ˎ below a word indicates low falling tune, while ˏ indicates low rising. Similar diacritics placed above a word indicate high falling or high rising tune. The diacritic ⌐ indicates a high pitch register for the whole tone group.

REFERENCES

Agrawal, A., 1976. Who Will Speak Next. *Papers in Linguistic Analysis, University of Delhi* 1 (1) : 58–70.

Aulakh, G., and R. Van Valin, 1977. Analysis of an Argument (Working Paper. Language Behavior Research Laboratory. University of California Berkeley).

Chafe, W., 1974. Language and Consciousness. *Language* 50 (1) : 111–133.

Cole, P., and J. L. Morgan, eds., 1975. *Syntax and Semantics, Speech Acts*, Vol. 3 (New York: Academic Press).

Crystal, D., 1975. *The English Tone of Voice* (London: Edward Arnold).

Erickson, Frederick, 1975. Gatekeeping and the Melting Pot: Interaction in Counseling Encounters: *Harvard Educational Review* 45 (1) : 44–70.

Gumperz, J. J., 1976. Language, Communication and Public Negotiation. In *Anthology and the Public Interest: Fieldwork and Theory*, P. Sanday, ed. (New York: Academic Press), pp. 273–292.

Gumperz, J. J., A. Agrawal, and G. Aulakh, 1977. Prosody, Paralinguistics and Contextualization in Indian English (Working Paper. Language Behavior Research Laboratory. University of California Berkeley).

Labov, W., 1973. *Language in the Inner City* (Philadelphia: University of Pennsylvania Press).

Lambert, W. E., 1972. *Language, Psychology, and Culture, Essays by Wallace E. Lambert* (Stanford, Cal.: Stanford University Press).

Shuy, R. W., W. A. Wolfram, and W. K. Riley, 1968. *Field Techniques in an Urban Language Study* (Washington, D.C.: Center for Applied Linguistics).

Turner, R., 1974. *Ethnomethodology* (Harmondsworth, England: Penguin).

The Anatomy of Language Diversity: Some Elementary Results

STANLEY LIEBERSON

One of the central aspects of racial and ethnic contact is the degree
to which language sets groups apart from one another.[1] Where mutual
intelligibility between groups is low, language is a major force for the
maintenance of ethnic divisions. Where ethnic or racial groups share a
common tongue, on the other hand, language provides a bridge between
these populations and is an important steppingstone toward the decline of
other group differences. There is a danger in overemphasizing the importance of language, since clearly groups can remain separate even if
they are not divided on linguistic lines. It is relevant, though, that a
shared language is necessary for the assimilation or merger of groups in
contact—even if it is not always a sufficient condition. Where populations
do not share the same tongue, communication channels along these language lines are necessarily restricted, and even groups that are in contact
do not share the same experiences or possess a very high degree of mutual intelligibility. Even if ethnic groups with different mother tongues are
bilingual, the ability to share the subtle nuances and communicate freely
is still restricted by the lack of a common mother tongue. This is the
essential message in Deutsch's notable effort to consider the role of language in the maintenance of ethnic groups (1953).

This chapter describes a basic procedure for analyzing the degree of
linguistic intelligibility possible between members of each ethnic group
studied, as well as between members of different ethnic groups. The procedure is designed to analyze the three fundamental influences on communication within any linguistically pluralistic situation, namely, each
group's mother tongue composition, bilingualism, and segregation or
other forms of nonrandom interaction. The concern here is clearly not
with measuring or analyzing the institutional, cultural, and normative
forces that generate these phenomena or alter them—for instance, government policies, the educational system, the work world, and economic
and political power. Regardless of the starting point, the effect of any of
these influences must be transferred through a change in one or more of
the characteristics under study here.

If, for example, the values of a group are such that its members are unusually tenacious about their language, then we would expect this to influence the isolation, or bilingualism, or mother tongue composition of the group. Similarly, if through economic changes stronger demands are made for fluency in a given tongue, the response will ultimately be an increase in bilingualism or in isolation. In addition, a group in process of linguistic shift will first exhibit a rise in bilingualism followed in turn by a change in mother tongue composition. My position, however, is that these three attributes are more than intervening variables; rather, they are also important causal considerations for interpreting the outcome of linguistic contact. Regardless of values, for example, the position of a language spoken by 87 percent of the population will somehow be much stronger than in another community where the same tongue is used by only 2 percent of the populace. Here we can intuitively see that holding all other factors constant in the two communities, the fundamental nature of the linguistic contact will be influenced by population composition.

This chapter consists of three parts. First, a method is presented for analyzing potential linguistic communication within an ethnic population or the total community or nation. Second, an analogous method is presented for potential linguistic communication between ethnic or racial groups. Finally, some applications of these techniques are presented in order to give the reader some illustrations of their potential value in the study of linguistic bonds within and between groups. In all of the illustrations, I will assume that there are two mother tongues represented in each group or community, designated as A and B, and that some members of each mother tongue are monolingual, designated by a subscript *o* for *only*. The subscript *a* designates those who speak A as a second language and *b* designates those who have learned B as a second tongue. Some of this may seem unnatural since there are situations where all members of a given ethnic group have a common mother tongue, or where no members are bilingual, but this example does provide all of the basic computations that would be involved in even more complicated multilingual social situations.

COMMUNICATION WITHIN A COMMUNITY OR GROUP: H_w

One of the simplest and most direct measures of potential speech in a shared tongue is H, the Index of Communication, proposed by Greenberg. This is "the probability that if two members of the population are

chosen at random, they will have at least one language in common"
(Greenberg 1956:112). H then is a basic statistical tool for describing
the degree to which a population can participate in mutually intelligible
speech. Its range runs from 1.00 (where every possible pair of speakers
share at least one common tongue) to 0 (the unlikely extreme where
every speaker possesses a different mother tongue and has not learned the
language of anyone else). It is expressed in operational form, a characteristic which has drawn praise from the statisticians Goodman and Kruskal
(1959:155), so that the probability of mutually intelligible speech can
be stated once the linguistic abilities of the population are known.

H_w is computed in the following way. Following Lieberson's terminology (1965:13), we will use the subscript w to label this measure of
linguistic communication within a population. Suppose there is a community (or an ethnic group) where two languages are used, so that 20
percent of the population are native speakers of A and 80 percent are
native speakers of B. Assume that some speakers of each mother tongue
have learned the second language of the community; in this case one-
fourth of the A speakers can also speak B and one-eighth of the B speakers can communicate in A. The subscript o is used to designate those
who speak only their mother tongue, a designates those who speak A as
a second tongue, and b designates members of the population who have
learned B as their second language. The community is divided proportionately as follows:

$$A_o = .15$$
$$B_o = .70$$
$$A_b = .05$$
$$B_a = .10$$
$$\text{Total} = 1.00$$

H_w is simply the proportion of all pairs of persons in which one or
more mutually intelligible tongue is shared. In this case,

$$H_w = (A_o)^2 + (B_o)^2 + (A_b + B_a)^2 + 2A_o(A_b + B_a) + 2B_o(A_b + B_a).$$

Thus $H_w = (.15)^2 + (.70)^2 + (.05 + .10)^2 + 2(.15)(.05 + .10)$
$+ 2(.70)(.05 + .10) = .79$. If two people are randomly selected
from the population, mutually intelligible communication will be possible
in 79 percent of the cases. In $1.00 - H_w$, or 21 percent of the time,
verbal communication between randomly interacting pairs will be impossible.

A given H_w can be achieved through different combinations of mono-
and bilingualism among a population. For example, if all of the As were
monolingual, $A_o = .20$, and if the Bs were distributed so that $B_o = .525$

and $B_a = .275$, then H_w would again be .79. As the example suggests, although the index describes the degree of mutually intelligible communication possible within a population, it fails to provide any information about the strength of each tongue, the relative degree of use in communication, and the separate impact on the monolingual and bilingual segment of each language group. To accomplish this, the simple situation is decomposed into the various components shown in Table 1.

First, observe that H_w is equal to the sum of components I, II, and III. In effect, communication occurs in one of three ways: through language A in situations where one or both speakers only know A (component I); through B when one or both speakers are able to use only B (II); and through either tongue where two bilingual speakers are in contact so that either language can be used (III). In the first two instances, a bilingual speaker must use the monolingual's language regardless of the former's preference if communication is to occur. Component IV gives the proportion of contact situations in which linguistic communication is impossible. This is a function of the relative sizes of the two monolingual groups, $1 - H = 2(A_o)(B_o)$. Making the fairly reasonable assumption that most bilinguals will use their mother tongue among

Table 1. Components of the H_w Index

Component	Description	Encounter Type	Formula	Illustration
I	A must be used	(a) A_oA_o	$(A_o)^2$	.0225
		(b) A_oA_b	$2(A_oA_b)$	.0150
		(c) A_oB_a	$2(A_oB_a)$	.0300
	Sum: $(A_o)^2 + 2A_o(A_b + B_a)$			.0675
II	B must be used	(a) B_oB_o	$(B_o)^2$	.4900
		(b) B_oB_a	$2(B_oB_a)$	.1400
		(c) B_oA_b	$2(B_oA_b)$	.0700
	Sum: $(B_o)^2 + 2B_o(B_a + A_b)$			.7000
III	Option (favoring A) (a) A_bA_b		$(A_b)^2$	.0025
	Option (favoring B) (b) B_aB_a		$(B_a)^2$	.0100
	Option (no clear preference)			
		(c) A_bB_a	$2(A_b)(B_a)$	.0100
	Sum: $(A_b)^2 + (B_a)^2 + 2(A_b)(B_a)$			.0225
Total probability of communication				.7900
IV	No communication possible			
		A_oB_o	$2(A_o)(B_o)$	.2100

NOTE: Illustration based on figures given in text for hypothetical situation.

other bilinguals with the same mother tongue, the optional component, III, can be divided into three subcategories: III_a, those cases of interaction where A will probably be favored; III_b, where B will be favored; III_c, those cases where bilinguals with different mother tongues are in contact and where no natural preference is evident. The sum of these three subcomponents total to III. The proportion of all contact situations in which A can be used is determined by the sum of components I and III; the proportion in which B can be used is the sum of II and III.

COMMUNICATION POTENTIAL
BETWEEN ETHNIC GROUPS: H_b

For either an ethnic group or community, the components of H_w presented in Table 1 provide a means for examining the communication potential existing at a given time as well as the ramifications for communication of any specified change in mother tongue composition or bilingualism. However, the H_w index does not determine the potential communication between the ethnic groups of a community, although it can be used to measure communication within these groups. Elsewhere, the author has shown why H_w cannot be employed in the analysis of communication between groups and, in addition, has proposed an index that is fully compatible with Greenberg's measure of within-group diversity (Lieberson 1964).

The solution essentially involves taking the linguistic distribution of each population and then determining the sum of cross-products between members of the two groups who share one or more common languages. This measure of potential communication between subpopulations, H_b, gives the probability that if one member is chosen at random from each of two populations they will have at least one language in common and therefore be able to speak to each other.

Suppose there are two languages, A and B, spoken in each ethnic group, I and J, and that bilingualism exists among members of both mother tongues. For the two groups, I and J, $H_b = I_{A_o} (J_{A_o} + J_{A_b} + J_{B_a}) + I_{B_o} (J_{B_o} + J_{B_a} + J_{A_b}) + I_{A_b} (J_{A_o} + J_{A_b} + J_{B_a} + J_{B_o}) + I_{B_a} (J_{A_o} + J_{A_b} + J_{B_o} + J_{B_a})$, where the subscripts indicate the proportion of the specified ethnic group with a given mother tongue (uppercase) and second tongue, if any (lowercase). Monolinguals are indicated by a lowercase o. Thus if $I_{A_o} = .15$, this means 15 percent of the I ethnic group have mother tongue A and are monolingual.

H_b, like H_w, has a range from 0 to 1, where 0 means no language is shared between speakers of the two groups and 1.0 would occur if all members of each ethnic group could speak to all members of the other group. Having introduced this additional measure, ethnic subscripts will distinguish between the two measures. Thus: H_i will refer to the H_w measure within ethnic group I; H_j will refer to H_w for ethnic group J; H_{ij} will refer to mutual intelligibility between the two groups; and H_{i+j} will refer to communication within the combined total population consisting of I and J members.

Table 2. Components of the H_{ij} Index

Component	Description	Encounter Type	Illustration
I	A must be used	(a) I_{A_0} J_{A_0}	.0375
		(b) I_{A_0} J_{A_b}	.0825
		(c) I_{A_0} J_{B_a}	.0000
		(d) I_{A_b} J_{A_0}	.0125
		(e) I_{B_a} J_{A_0}	.0250
	Sum: $I_{A_0} (J_{A_0} + J_{A_b} + J_{B_a}) + J_{A_0} (I_{A_b} + I_{B_a})$		.1575
II	B must be used	(a) I_{A_b} J_{B_0}	.0100
		(b) I_{B_a} J_{B_0}	.0200
		(c) I_{B_0} J_{A_b}	.3850
		(d) I_{B_0} J_{B_a}	.0000
		(e) I_{B_0} J_{B_0}	.1400
	Sum: $I_{B_0} (J_{A_b} + J_{B_a} + J_{B_0}) + J_{B_0} (I_{A_b} + I_{B_a})$		.5550
III	Option (favoring A)	(a) I_{A_b} J_{A_b}	.0275
	Option (favoring B)	(b) I_{B_a} J_{B_a}	.0000
	Option (no clear preference)	(c) I_{A_b} J_{B_a}	.0000
	Option (no clear preference)	(d) I_{B_a} J_{A_b}	.0550
	Sum: $I_{B_a} (J_{B_a} + J_{A_b}) + I_{A_b} (J_{A_b} + J_{B_a})$		.0825
Total probability of communication			.7950
IV	No communication possible	(a) I_{A_0} J_{B_0}	.0300
		(b) I_{B_0} J_{A_0}	.1750
	Sum:		.2050

NOTE: Encounter type and formulas are identical and hence not shown separately. Illustration based on figures given below for hypothetical situation:

	I	J
A_0	.15	.25
B_0	.70	.20
A_b	.05	.55
B_a	.10	.00
Total	1.00	1.00

Based on the hypothetical language distributions shown at the bottom of Table 2, an example is provided of the computation of the index for potential communication between members of ethnic groups I and J. As was the case for H_w, the H_{ij} index is equal to the sum of three components: communication through language A in circumstances where one or both people speak only A, communication through language B in analogous circumstances for language B, and where communication is possible in either tongue because both the I and J ethnic group members are bilingual. The two subcomponents where no mutually shared language is held are also indicated.

One consequence of obtaining the H_i, H_j, and H_{ij} measures is that communication potential within each of the ethnic groups, respectively I and J, may be compared with the potential between groups. This enables one to measure the role of language as a bond setting off the ethnic groups from one another as well as its cohesive force within each group. Of particular interest is the degree of communication possible within and between the ethnic groups with and without bilingualism. The latter, based on just the mother tongue composition of the groups, may be easily measured with procedures discussed elsewhere. Computing the A index for mother tongue diversity—described in Greenberg (1956) for measurement within an ethnic group and in Lieberson (1964) for measurement between ethnic groups—it is only necessary that the index so obtained be subtracted from 1.0 to obtain a value that is exactly analogous to the H indexes described here. In an application based on various Canadian cities, the result is that often the mother tongue bond is stronger between the French and British ethnic groups than it is within the French group. Bilingualism in a number of these cases has the surprising quality of raising within-group communication potential more rapidly than raising the potential for communication between ethnic groups (see Lieberson 1970: 241–245).

SOME IMPLICATIONS

Three serious questions about these procedures should be considered. First, are there data that can be applied to these analytical techniques? Second, given the complex set of factors that affect language behavior— for instance, power, values, work pressures, mobility, and the like—are these procedures so oversimplified that they are of little value in understanding the role of language in the bonds within and between ethnic or racial groups? Third, what do they tell us about linguistic issues that are not evident from the tabulations themselves?

As for the first question, not only are there census data for several countries that provide information on mother tongue and bilingualism— Cyprus, India, and Canada, for example—but any sociolinguistic or ethnic study having field research that entailed gathering data on the language skills of the population would provide data applicable to these techniques. I have no doubt that there will be an increasing number of this type of data sets.

As for the second question, it is of course true that a complex set of factors affects the language patterns of ethnic groups in contact. The analytical procedures outlined in the two tables, however, do enable one to determine the consequences for within- and between-group communication potential under any observed or hypothetical set of conditions. One can determine, for example, the consequences of any set of changes in mother tongue composition (due, for example, to migration) or in bilingualism (due to new industrial requirements or changes in the educational opportunity structure) or in segregation (such that members of a given group change the frequency with which they are in contact with other segments of the community in terms of where they work or live or attend school). These are powerful tools, even if the underlying causes are not directly measured, insofar as the procedures permit some consideration of the consequences that develop.

As for the implications of these components, I have listed some below that I find either not to be obvious or, if so, to be important enough that a formal proof is valuable in understanding the role of language in ethnic relations.

Mother tongue composition. The consequence of a change in mother tongue composition is different for communication within an ethnic group (the H_i or H_j measure) as opposed to communication between ethnic groups (H_{ij}). A unit change in mother tongue composition due to migration, mortality, fertility, intergenerational shift, or other factors will have varying effects on communication potential within a population. For example, if there is a community where half of the populace are As and the other half Bs, then a shift of the nature that 60 percent of the population are Bs will have relatively little influence on the degree of mutually intelligible communication in the community. In this case, H_w would rise from .50 to .52, a change of .02. By contrast, in a community where 80 percent are monolingual As and 20 percent B_os, a change to a situation where 90 percent are A_os would raise H_w from .68 to .82, a rise of .14. In short, a change in a community where most members share a common mother tongue will have a more severe impact on overall communication than a change of equal magnitude in a community with a lower initial H_w.

By contrast, unit changes in mother tongue composition have a constant effect on the level of interethnic communication potential. This leads to a curious paradox: a given change in a group's mother tongue composition will not necessarily have the same consequences for within- and between-group communication potential. Indeed, as far as within-group communication is concerned, shifts in mother tongue composition have a changing impact on communication potential.[2]

Bilingualism. Rather clearly, communication potential within a group will rise as bilingualism increases. Where all other factors are constant, H_w-type indexes will change in accordance with the degree of bilingualism among the mother tongue populations. Less obvious are some quantitative relationships between bilingualism and mutual intelligibility. In the simple situation where only two mother tongues are present, shifts of equal magnitude between the bilingual and monolingual segments of a given mother tongue population have an impact on H_w, which is a function of the mother tongue composition of the community and the degree of bilingualism among the mother tongue group held constant.

Following component IV presented earlier in Table 1, we recognize that $H_w = 1.00 - 2A_0B_0$. Since B_0 and 2 are constant regardless of the initial level of A_0, a unit change in A_0 will have a constant effect on H_w, which is a function of $2B_0$. Thus a unit change in bilingualism among a given mother tongue group leads to a unit change in H_w regardless of the initial degree of bilingualism in the population undergoing a shift.

To put this into applied terms, visualize two cities in Canada; the proportion of the population who are monolingual B speakers and bilingual Bs is the same in both. However, nearly all the As in one city are bilingual while almost no As in the second city can speak B. If an equal number of monolingual As in the two cities now learn B, the H_w indexes for the two communities will rise equally—although they differ in their initial positions. A rise from 85 percent to 100 percent bilingualism among As will increase H_w as much as an equal rise from 0 to 15 percent bilingualism among As in the second city.

A second observation about the relation between bilingualism and communication within a population is that the influence on H_w of unit shifts in bilingualism among one mother tongue population will vary in accordance with the degree of bilingualism among the mother tongue group held constant. *The greater the degree of monolingualism among one speech group, the smaller the total communication within the community or society, holding everything else constant. However, the greater will be the rise in communication with a unit increase in bilingualism among the other mother tongue population.*

This indicates that the effect of an equal degree of bilingualism will vary with the mother tongue composition of the community *and* with the group that is bilingual. Let A be the smaller mother tongue group, so that A < B; let K be the number of people who are bilingual; further, let K ≦ A. Then H_w will be highest where all the bilinguals K have mother tongue A. H_w will be the lowest where all the bilinguals are members of mother tongue B. And H_w will vary directly with A_b/K. This is shown in Table 3, where the 5 percent of the population that are bilinguals are shifted so that: first, all bilinguals are As; second, all bilinguals are Bs; and finally, half of the bilinguals are As and half are Bs. The range of H_w varies from .76 to .70 depending on which group are the bilinguals. More generally, holding population composition constant as well as the percentage of the community who are bilingual, H_w will go up as the bilingual component shifts from the larger group to the smaller.

A striking quantitative implication of this general statement deals with the degree of bilingualism in each group necessary to yield the same H_w. The H_w obtained when a given percent of the larger mother tongue group is bilingual will equal the H_w obtained when the same percent of the smaller mother tongue group is bilingual. This means that where there is a considerable difference in size between the two language groups, it will take a far greater number of bilinguals among the larger group to yield the same degree of mutual intelligibility within the community. In terms of minimizing effort, if we ignore difficulties in learning languages, the optimum means for raising mutual intelligibility through bilingualism is by having only the smaller mother tongue group become bilingual. Implications of this finding for underdeveloped areas and other nations endeavoring to formulate a national language policy are clear-cut. While there are many other factors for planners and statesmen to consider, it is readily possible to draw out a program for obtaining a given level of mutual intelligibility that involves the minimum degree of second-language learning.

Table 3. Variations in the Effect of Bilingualism on Communication Potential Within a Community

Linguistic Component	A is bilingual	B is bilingual	A and B are bilingual
A_o	.15	.20	.175
B_o	.80	.75	.775
A_b	.05	0	.025
B_a	0	.05	.025
H_w	.76	.70	.729

It is important to recognize that the degree of bilingualism in each mother tongue group will fluctuate over time. Assuming again that A is the smaller of the two mother tongue groups, on the basis of earlier observations we would expect net changes in bilingualism among a given number of A speakers to alter the degree of intelligibility more than a change of the same number among the B mother tongue group. This means that the importance of shifts in bilingualism for the total community will vary in accordance with the mother tongue group involved. It is possible to state the exact increase in bilingualism necessary among one mother tongue group to compensate for a decline in bilingualism among the other speech group. Similarly, if a group increases its bilingualism, it is easy to determine the drop in bilingualism that can occur among speakers of the second mother tongue without a decline in H_w. If we define A_o' as the number speaking A_o after a shift and B_o' as the number speaking B_o after a shift, then these four rules apply to all two-language contact situations:

If K people shift from A_b to A_o, then the number of B_o who must become bilingual to maintain H_w at its previous level is:

$$B_o - \frac{(A_o)\,(B_o)}{B_o'}.$$

If K people shift from A_o to A_b, the number of B_a who can become monolingual without a decline in H_w is:

$$\frac{(A_o)\,(B_o)}{A_o'} - B_o.$$

If K people shift from B_a to B_o, then the number of A_o who must become bilingual to maintain H_w at its previous level is:

$$A_o - \frac{(A_o)\,(B_o)}{B_o'}.$$

If K people shift from B_o to B_a, the number of A_b who can become monolingual without a decline in H_w is:

$$\frac{(A_o)\,(B_o)}{B_o'} - A_o.$$

To illustrate the application of these formulas, consider a population of 1,000 with an initial linguistic distribution as follows: A_o is 150, A_b is 50, B_o is 700, and B_a is 100. The proportional distribution among the four language components is respectively .15, .05, .70, and .10, with an H_w index of .79. Suppose the monolingual B mother tongue population declines by 140 such that B_o is now 560 and B_a is 240. Given this increase in bilingualism among the B population, how large a number of A_b speakers could shift to A_o without dropping the H_w index? Applying the last of the four equations shown above, the number equals:

$$\frac{(A_o)(B_o)}{B_o'} - A_o, \text{ thus } \frac{(150)(700)}{560} - 150,$$

which equals 37.5. This is .0375 of the population. Hence, given that B_o has become .56 and B_a is .24, H_w would remain unchanged if A_o increases to .1875 (.15 + .0375) and A_b drops to .0125 (.05 − .0375).

Communication within and between ethnic groups. If there are two ethnic groups, two mother tongues in each group, no bilingualism, and the largest mother tongue in each ethnic group is different, then communication within each ethnic population will inevitably exceed communication across ethnic lines, that is, H_{ij} will be less than either H_i or H_j. For example, if $A = .9$ and $B = .1$ for ethnic group I, and $A = .1$ and $B = .9$ for the J group, then H_{ij} will be only .18 whereas H_i and H_j will both be .82.

The exact relationship between H_{ij} and the linguistic composition of ethnic groups I and J may be determined in the two-language–monolingual context on the basis of the following formula:

$$H_{ij} = .50 + (I_A - I_B)(J_A - .50),$$

where I_A is the proportion of ethnic group I with mother tongue A; I_B is the proportion of ethnic group I with mother tongue B; J_A is the proportion of ethnic group J with mother tongue A. This formula shows the effect of changes in the linguistic composition of one group on intergroup communication when the composition of the second ethnic group remains constant. The formula also applies, incidentally, to cases where the largest mother tongue is the same in each of the two ethnic groups.

If the largest mother tongue is different in the two groups, out-group communication will be only slightly less than in-group communication when both H_i and H_j are relatively low. When in-group communication is very high for both groups, then out-group communication will be low both in an absolute sense and in comparison to the degree of mutual intelligibility within each group.

Contact settings where the numerically largest mother tongue is the same for each ethnic group are also of interest. In cases of linguistic assimilation, we would expect to find an intermediate stage where the same mother tongue is most important in each group, but where a sizable minority of the assimilating group still retains the old mother tongue. Under such conditions, the assimilating group will actually have lower mutual intelligibility among themselves than with the second ethnic population. Where two ethnic populations differ in their mother tongue composition but both have the same numerically dominant mother tongue, then with no bilingualism we will find $H_i > H_{ij} > H_j$, if I is the ethnic group that is more homogeneous linguistically. Where two groups share the same dominant mother tongue, but in different degrees, the situation will be one in which a decline will be expected in linguistic unity among the more heterogeneous group in the sense that communication within J will be lower than the communication potential that J members have with the I group. Observe, of course, that this does not hold for ethnic group I since their in-group communication potential exceeds the potential for that across ethnic boundaries. Where linguistic assimilation has proceeded far enough so that the group's most important tongue is the same as that of the other group, we can see how tenuous unity within the assimilating group becomes.

In view of the important differences between contact settings where the largest mother tongue is the same in both ethnic groups and those settings where different mother tongues are dominant, we shall refer to the former as "shared dominance" and the latter as "distinctive dominance." In shared dominance settings, linguistic unity within the less homogeneous ethnic group is actually lower than it is with the other ethnic group. In distinctive dominance settings, both ethnic groups always have higher within-group than between-group mutual intelligibility.

Bilingualism. Acquisition of a second language by some members of an ethnic group will raise the potential for both in-group communication (assuming that not all members share the same mother tongue) and also raise H between the ethnic groups. The first question to ask is whether in-group or out-group communication is raised more rapidly by bilingualism. No flat answer can be given; rather, the mother tongue composition of the two groups determines if H_i or H_{ij} increases more rapidly when bilingualism occurs among some members of the I group.

The techniques presented in this paper allow one to analyze the implications of the various possible situations. Consider a setting where only two mother tongues are found and where all second-language learning occurs in these languages. Under these circumstances, a change in monolingualism can only occur through an opposite change in the bilingual segment able to speak both tongues. First, we can define our H measures as follows:

$$H_i = 1 - 2\,(I_{A_o})\,(I_{B_o}),$$
$$H_j = 1 - 2\,(J_{A_o})\,(J_{B_o}),$$
$$H_{ij} = 1 - [(I_{A_o})\,(J_{B_o}) + (I_{B_o})\,(J_{A_o})].$$

Using Delta to indicate a change in value from an earlier status, we can see that a change in I_{A_0} will have the following effect:

Delta H_i = Delta I_{A_0} ($2 I_{B_0}$),
Delta H_{ij} = Delta I_{A_0} (J_{B_0}).

Therefore, we conclude that bilingualism among members of I will raise H_{ij} more rapidly than H_i only under the following conditions:

If I_{A_b} increases, H_{ij} will rise more rapidly when $J_B > 2I_B$.
If I_{B_a} increases, H_{ij} will rise more rapidly when $J_A > 2I_A$.

Of course, were both the A- and B-speaking members of an ethnic group all to become bilingual, then H_i would equal H_{ij} since communication would be possible in all cases. For analytical purposes, however, it is advisable to restrict ourselves to the situation where members of only one linguistic segment of an ethnic group become bilingual. In terms of practical application, the formulas given above are extremely important for contact settings where there is distinctive dominance, i.e., where the dominant mother tongue is different in the two ethnic groups. If I's dominant tongue is A and J's dominant tongue is B, then the learning of a second language by the I_{A_0} population could undermine linguistic unity in I only if $J_B < 2I_B$. What this means is that bilingualism among the dominant mother tongue of one ethnic group has an impact on the relative rise of in-group versus out-group communication which depends on the compositional conditions indicated above. On the one hand, in-group unity may actually rise more rapidly than out-group unity even when the other group's dominant mother tongue is learned by the second ethnic population. Under other circumstances, bilingualism can sharply undercut the degree language provides a unifying force for the ethnic groups.

A second question follows from the answer to the first: namely, in those distinctive dominance settings where out-group communication rises more rapidly than in-group communication, with sufficient bilingualism can the H_{ij} index actually exceed H_i? The answer is no, at least under the conditions where only one mother tongue segment of an ethnic group becomes bilingual. Although the more rapid rise in intergroup communication potential through bilingualism will lead to a decline in the differential, which in some cases may be considerable, linguistic potential will never be lower within the groups whose members become bilingual than across ethnic lines.

Segregation. The limitations of space do not permit a thorough mathematical consideration here of the linguistic consequences of segregation. Whether one examines residential location, work situations, or other contact settings, it is clear that racial and ethnic groups tend to be segregated. It is also clear that such forms of segregation reduce the needs for communication across ethnic lines and, in turn, thereby reduce to some unknown degree the need to acquire a second language. As a consequence, segregation can be viewed as an alternative to bilingualism. How much of an alternative is a moot point, but it is at least in part affected by the groups' mother tongue composition. Although he works from a somewhat different perspective, Coleman's examination of segregation is of interest here. He finds that size of group has a bearing on the magnitude of segregation necessary for members of the group to attain a certain frequency of interaction with compatriots (Coleman 1964: 484–487). As one might expect, there is an inverse linkage such that less segregation is required as the group's relative size increases. If one postulates some minimal level of communication potential needed at a given stage of industrial and social development, the ability of groups to isolate themselves instead of (or as a partial alternative to) becoming bilingual will vary directly with the group's size. On the other hand, the pressure to become bilingual, holding such forces as political power and economic dominance constant, will vary inversely with group size. Accordingly, it should be possible to work out curves whereby one can determine the magnitude of segregation necessary as an alternative to a given level of bilingualism for a specific mother tongue situation.

Regarding segregation, one should also note the incredible complexity that may exist when there are linguistic differences among members of each ethnic group. In a simple situation where there are two mother tongues represented within an ethnic group, there will be four separate linguistic subclasses; that is, there can be both bilingual and monolingual speakers of each of the two mother tongues among members of a single ethnic group. Under these circumstances, the frequency of ethnic interaction does not necessarily correspond to the degree of mutual intelligibility—indeed they may very well run in opposite directions. A dilemma exists for some linguistic components of an ethnic group since the optimal form of ethnic interaction is not the optimal means for maximizing linguistic contact and, likewise, the optimal form of linguistic interaction reduces the degree of contact with ethnic compatriots from the maximum possible. Consider, for example, the ethnolinguistic situation in Montreal. Since the mother tongue of the French ethnic population is predominantly French, communication for the small number of French ethnics with an English mother tongue would hardly be raised through the maximization of contact with their ethnic compatriots. The interaction pattern among English mother tongue members of the French ethnic population would also depend on whether they had acquired French as a second language. Far more significant numerically is the behavior of the sizable bilingual and monolingual segments of the French mother tongue component. Since bilingual French Canadians have no need to interact with French Canadians in order to maximize their degree of mutual intelligibility, a very important consideration is whether the bilinguals differ from monolinguals in their patterns of linguistic and ethnic association. Analogous questions could be asked about Montrealers of British origin or of any other ethnic group whose members differ in mother tongue or acquired languages.

The point is that the linguistic components of each ethnic group may vary greatly in their optimal strategies for maximizing intelligibility and contacts with ethnic compatriots. Moreover, if we postulate some maximum segregation ratio possible for each ethnolinguistic segment of a community (that is, the component of an ethnic group with identical linguistic capabilities) then we will find that often the groups face a dilemma in the alternatives available to them. Even without considering the maximum self-selection possible, however, the groups face alternatives in the degree linguistic communication or ethnic contact is maximized.

CONCLUSION

The techniques presented allow one to analyze mathematically the role of language as a bond both between and within ethnic groups. It must be emphasized that these techniques do not allow one to deal with ultimate causes. Nevertheless, they provide analytical tools for examining the implications that any and all mother tongue and bilingual situations have for ethnic unity. Although only touched upon here, very likely the next expansion of this procedure is an analysis of the ethnolinguistic impact of segregation in various domains such as residence, work, education, and other institutions.

NOTES

1. The support of the Ford Foundation, Grant 755-0669, is gratefully acknowledged.
2. I have not attempted to provide the algebraic proofs in this paper, but the interested reader may determine the nature of the relationships by inspecting formulas shown in Tables 1 and 2 or experimenting with a hypothetical data set.

REFERENCES

Coleman, James S., 1964. *Introduction to Mathematical Sociology* (New York: Free Press).
Deutsch, Karl W., 1953. *Nationalism and Social Communication* (Cambridge: Technology Press of the Massachusetts Institute of Technology).
Greenberg, Joseph H., 1956. The Measurement of Linguistic Diversity. *Language* 32 : 109–115.
Goodman, Leo A., and William H. Kruskal, 1959. Measures of Association for Cross Classifications, II: Further Discussion and References. *Journal of the American Statistical Association* 54 : 123–163.
Lieberson, Stanley, 1964. An Extension of Greenberg's Linguistic Diversity Measures. *Language* 40 : 526–531.
————, 1965. Bilingualism in Montreal: A Demographic Analysis. *American Journal of Sociology* 71 : 10–25.
————, 1970. *Language and Ethnic Relations in Canada* (New York: John Wiley).

Communication Patterns:
Some Aspects of Nonverbal Behavior
in Intercultural Communication

FATHI S. YOUSEF

In intercultural communication many misunderstandings are the result of misinterpreted behaviors. Three social behavior patterns in intercultural communication contexts are presented, discussed, and analyzed in this chapter. The areas studied are guest-host relationships, notions about masculinity and femininity, and orientations toward old age. The themes are presented in three case studies delineating different situational behaviors. The situations are analyzed and the patterns are drawn, examined, and interpreted. In every situation, from the cultural perspectives of each of the persons, the behavior of the others seems rather strange and ranges from the weird to the downright unacceptable. At all times, however, each person considers his or her own behavior to be meaningful and "proper."

CASE STUDIES IN SITUATIONAL BEHAVIOR

I: A Gift For The Baby! John and Mary Ford live in a middle-class neighborhood in St. Paul, Minnesota. They are both junior college instructors and have just returned from their first trip overseas. In three weeks they visited Spain, Tunisia, Austria, Italy, and Greece. John and Mary are excited when they find out that the house next door has been sold to a Lebanese surgeon and his wife who have just emigrated to the United States. Mike and Mona Kalb in the meantime are glad to find that their new neighbors, John and Mary, are quite friendly. John and Mary think that the world would be a terrific place if only people could travel and get to meet and know each other. A month later John and Mary learn that Mona has returned home from the hospital after delivering a baby girl. The new parents are congratulated, and on the weekend John and Mary take a gift for the baby and go to visit Mike and Mona. When they arrive John and Mary find another couple there, a cousin of Mike and his wife. Mary gives Mona the baby's gift, which Mona accepts thankfully. Then introductions are made, and all sit down in the living room. Meanwhile, before Mona sits down she takes the wrapped gift and leaves it in the bedroom. The gift is not opened and no reference is made to it during the visit. On the way out, however, at the door, Mike and Mona profusely thank John and Mary for their kindness, thoughtfulness, and consideration in bringing them such a fantastic gift for the baby. When Mary says that she hopes the gift will be useful and that she bought it according to her mother's recommendation, Mike and Mona in the same breath assure her that it certainly will be.

On the way home, Mary turns to John and says:

"Aren't these people funny? I don't think they even cared to open the gift!"

"Yeah! Even though you distinctly asked if she wouldn't look at it."

At the same time they both laugh uneasily and say:

"Oh! Well! These foreigners!"

II: Is He Or Isn't He? Marsha Johnson and Juan Lopez are engaged and plan to be married soon. They are both seniors in a midwestern university in the United States. They met on campus and have been going together for a year. Marsha is from Des Moines, Iowa, and Juan is a foreign student from Costa Rica. Lately, Juan and Marsha have attended several social functions where there were many foreign students. Marsha has been bothered by the amount of physical contact in interaction between Juan and his male Latin American, Middle Eastern, and southern European friends. Marsha has never doubted Juan's masculinity. In fact, once alone with Juan she's been having a hard time trying to adjust to what she calls his manic sensuality. Seeing her fiancé hold a male friend's hand in public while they are talking, however, or walk down the hall arm in arm with another male friend somehow disturbs her, even though that often happens indoors or during social functions. Adding to her consternation is the fact that, for example, when she is standing next to Juan while he is talking to a friend, both guys will talk to her, yet, when they talk to each other, they both seem unable to interact without patting and touching each other!

Marsha is rather embarrassed about her feelings because she has taken a course in nonverbal behavior, in which she learned that people in Latin America, the Middle East, and southern Europe are quite tactile and require less space in their interactions. Marsha, along with some of her friends in the class, actually thought that this was interesting and cute and that it displayed warmth in human interaction. Yet, somehow, she finds now that that involvement with all these foreign behaviors is rather confusing, if not outright disconcerting. She has even been considering writing a letter to the editor of the advice column in the local paper in the hope that Juan would read it. After all, "When in Rome, do as the Romans do," but then, the irritating behaviors happened only during social functions.

"Oh! It is all so confusing!" she finds herself saying all the time.

III: Unfit To Live! Helen and Edward Thompson are two successful California attorneys in their middle thirties. They are both involved and active members in the life of their community. Through a YMCA program Grace Sibanda, a foreign student from Zambia, spends a week with them during Christmas vacation. They all take to each other very quickly.

Grace is impressed by the elegance of the house and the luxury of all the appliances that the Thompsons have. Grace thinks that the family must be rich. They have two cars, no children, and live in a nice neighborhood.

The Thompsons learn that Grace is the eldest of six children, that she is engaged to a distant cousin, and that she would be married when she went home after graduation. Asked about her future home, Grace tells the Thompsons that she would be living with her husband and his parents, who are old and ailing. When the Thompsons suggest that maybe Grace wouldn't like living with her husband's parents, Grace laughs nervously and explains that her fiancé is the only son of his parents and that, anyway, she isn't that kind of girl!

Later on, after that Christmas vacation, Grace discusses the situation with a Zambian friend and says:

"Do you know what surprised me most? Those people seemed so rich, yet the man's mother who is seventy years old lived in a nursing home. Both the man and his wife told me that. They even sounded happy and proud about it."

"Maybe they weren't really rich. My God, I don't think I would be fit to live if I let something like that happen to my parents!"

ANALYSIS OF SITUATIONS

In all of these case studies the people enter every interaction with feelings of compassion, interest, and care for each other and come out baffled, confused, or frustrated. In every situation each individual behaves according to the norms of his or her own cultural background and tries to be understanding and nonjudgmental. Still, in every case, the intercultural interaction leaves the naive participants puzzled and uncomfortable. The initial good feelings at the beginning of each relationship give way at the end to polite confusion and well-mannered indifference.

John and Mary Ford are considerate and friendly people. They are genuinely interested in their Lebanese neighbors. Yet, the Fords cannot help feeling slightly confused at the way their neighbors treat the baby's gift. To the Fords, there is something slightly diffident and irritating about the way their neighbors accept the baby's gift, and there is also something rather unusual and phony about the way the neighbors thank them for the gift. It is as if Mike and Mona Kalb are embarrassed at receiving that gift. Since it is obvious to the Fords that the package was not opened, the expressions of appreciation seem to them to be quite exaggerated.

On the other hand, Mike and Mona Kalb are happy about their neighbors' visit and touched by their thoughtfulness in bringing a gift to the new baby. The gift, however, is put away quickly, thankfully, and quietly and is not referred to during the Ford's visit. Mike and Mona do not mean to ignore the gift, they are simply following the norms of their own culture. There are two dimensions involved in the situation. First, when John and Mary arrive, the Kalbs already have company and do not feel it is proper to comment on the new gift that the guests have brought with them. Comments on the gift, though pleasing to the givers, might be embarrassing to others present who may not have brought gifts. Also, and the second dimension is related to the first, gifts in the Middle East are not only symbols of care, friendship, and thoughtfulness, but they reflect primarily in terms of value and material being the position and status of the giver and his or her relationship to the receiver. Hence, in quietly putting away the gift and not discussing or opening it in public, Mike and Mona are being mindful of the feelings of their company.

In the Middle East the exchange of gifts reflects the societal pattern of relationships. People interact and relate to each other in class-conscious vertical hierarchies of hereditary, financial, political, and occupational positions in society. Gifts are exchanged not in a *quid pro quo* pattern but rather according to the status in the hierarchy of the two parties. Status determines each side's expectations and obligations in the ongoing relationships. A gift also does not only reflect the current position and status of the giver but, at the same time, it shows how the giver likes to be considered in terms of upward or downward social mobility. Consequently, the actual material value of the gift is important in the interaction. The gift is thus a declaration of status and a fulfillment of obligations where one gives not in terms of "it's the thought that counts" but according to one's position in the hierarchy. The higher the position, the greater the obligations and expectations in terms of looking after others who are at rungs lower than one's own.

The system is an accepted vertical hierarchy of relationships where people on different rungs of the social structure are expected to extend attention, care, and patronage to those below them while they compete socially and in largesse with their peers and at the same time try through service and work to elevate themselves and curry favor with those in higher strata. It is a state of accepted and expected social interdependence in a vertical hierarchy where people are aware of their positions and the degrees of mobility they are permitted in the structure.

This system is unlike the situation in the United States, where the emphasis is on an assumed horizontal structure of relationships where all are avowedly equal and where every child has a chance to rise from rags to riches and from poverty to the presidency. In the cultural environment of the United States, for instance, people relate to each other on equal footing, and friendships and human relations in general are marked by independence rather than interdependence.

In the United States the question of face is of secondary importance; in the Middle East, the questions of shame and face underlie all interpersonal relations. Mike and Mona Kalb's concern about the maintenance of social amenities make them avoid the subject of the baby's gift. The hosts do not want to embarrass John and Mary Ford or the company already there. One couple might have brought the baby a gift when the other couple did not. Or, if both brought gifts, one gift might be higher or lower in value than the other. Showing the gifts then would publicly assign different statuses to the givers. Consequently, from a Middle Eastern cultural perspective, where people are keenly sensitive to the question of face, it is best to put the gift thankfully and quietly away. Later on, when alone with the giver, the hosts can express their gratitude.

Avoidance of the subject of the gift makes the North American guests feel confused; moreover, the profuse thanks of the hosts sound spurious. The hosts, Mike and Mona Kalb, though linguistically competent in English, are responding and reacting in terms of their cultural background, where linguistic exaggeration is the standard (Shouby 1951). Unlike English, where understatement is often laudable, in Arabic overstatement is the norm. While the speaker of English says, "Thank you," for instance, the native speaker of Arabic says, "A thousand, thousand thanks." An English notion like "It's improbable" would be expressed by the Arabic speaker as "It's definitely impossible!"

Notions about masculinity and femininity are reflected in the second situation, in the relationship of Marsha Johnson and Juan Lopez. On the cognitive level, Marsha is aware of the nature, meaning, and implications of proxemics and touching in crosscultural communication (Yousef 1968). She has even studied, enjoyed, and participated in class exercises on the subject. Actually, Marsha has thought of herself as a culturally aware person. She has felt even more assured since Juan has always complimented her knowledge of certain nuances of cross-cultural behavior. Experientially, however, Marsha finds that it is difficult to approve and be part of behaviors that she has always believed to be improper and unacceptable. The fact that Juan would let go of her hand at a social function when one of his male Latin, Middle Eastern, or southern European friends would come to talk to them, perhaps even would end up holding the arm or hand of the male friend, was disturbing to her. Marsha often wondered what her family would think of that.

Lately, Marsha has often teased Juan and his friends about their holding hands and hugging and kissing each other on the cheek when they met. Though she expressed understanding, she told them that she hoped they were aware that in the United States these behaviors were generally considered signs of homosexuality. They never seemed to mind. They always agreed, laughed, and said that nobody ever touched them on the butt, though. The comment did not make sense to Marsha. One could not question the masculinity of a behavior that super athletes and football stars engage in, such as patting each other on the buttocks to express support and admiration for a good play. She rationalized it, however, as a point of cultural difference when she was told that any male in Latin America, the Middle East, or southern Europe who allowed other males to pat him on the buttocks was being insulted, to put it mildly, and was being treated as a sissy.

At the same time Juan has been quite proud of his behavior toward Marsha, his fiancée. Unlike other North American girls he had dated before, this was the girl he was going to marry. He has always treated her with special respect in public, especially in front of friends and family. To him she was not a "cheap" girl, and, of course, he would never engage her in any public displays of amorous behavior, particularly in the presence of other male friends. If he did, she would be thought of and treated as "one of those girls"—daring, loose, and available! In any social function, therefore, if he finds he is holding Marsha's waist or hand when a male friend approaches them, Juan lets go of Marsha and moves imperceptibly a little farther from her. From his cultural perspective, Juan's nonverbal message to his male friends is that that girl is different and special.

In cross-cultural relationships, manifestations of masculinity and femininity can be rather confusing when considered apart from a society's underlying value system and behavior patterns. In Latin America, the Middle East, and southern Europe, strong societal notions of honor and shame are centered on the role and behavior of the female in the culture (Peristiany 1965). A woman's sexual behavior does not only affect and reflect on the woman concerned, but it influences the honor, position, and status of her immediate and extended family in the society. Public male-female touching is discouraged and frowned upon (Yousef 1976). Male-female greeting behavior between close relatives and friends, for example, is usually limited to handshakes or exchanged kisses on the cheeks. Overt behaviors that have direct sexual connotations or implications are avoided in public. "Good" girls are careful of their reputations. Male members of such societies jealously feel responsible for and guard the honor of the females in their immediate and extended families and clans. Honor is considered by all to be an entity that derives its main roots from the sexual behavior of the women in the family and clan. Damage to a girl's honor or reputation brings direct or indirect shame and disgrace to all who are associated with her or closely or remotely related to her. And the closer the relationship to a disgraced woman, the worse the damage to the position and prospects. Thus "innocent" greeting behaviors such as a hug and a short kiss on the lips between male and female friends or relatives in the United States is condemned in these societies, which invest heavily in the legal purity of the sexual behavior of their females.

According to these cultural standards, Juan Lopez thinks he is being considerate and mindful of his fiancée's reputation when he refrains from engaging her in public displays of affection, especially in front of people or friends who know them. "Real" men do not give the impression that their women are interested in activities that could have sexual connotations. That would be tantamount to saying the woman is unbridled and immoral. In the meantime, Marsha Johnson cannot help feeling a slight sense of rejection every time Juan lets go of her in public and moves a little closer to talk to a male friend.

In the third situation, in talking with Grace Sibanda, Helen and Edward Thompson reflect different orientations toward age and the role and place of the elderly in different societies. The ideas, behaviors, and beliefs of the Thompsons are reflections of the youth-oriented culture of the United States with its emphasis on independence and the nuclear family structure, while Grace Sibanda presents an orientation that values old age and interdependence and emphasizes the extended family structure.

The Thompsons are examples of success, American style. They met in their senior year in college, fell in love, and married. They both graduated *magna cum laude*. Helen went to work full time and supported Ed through law school. Ed passed the bar exam and joined a successful practice. Meantime, Helen went to law school and studied for her bar exam. It was a hard, busy life full of challenges to conquer. Recently, they started to enjoy the fruits of material success. They also started to get more involved in the life of their community. They have been excited about the YMCA program through which they met Grace Sibanda.

In their discussions with Grace, however, the Thompsons often feel "funny" about some of Grace's reactions. It seems as if Grace does not want or expect to have a home of her own away from her in-laws, nor does it sound as if her fiancé cares for the idea. Grace even seems to act as if the idea of her own home is an unbecoming thought that should not be attributed to her, especially since she explains that her fiancé is an only son. Later the Thompsons wonder at how a bright, young girl like Grace, who is obviously ambitious enough to study for a master's degree in public administration, seems to have no sense of independence. When the Thompsons also learned that Grace's fiancé is a British-educated physician who does not consider the idea of moving away from his family's home after marriage, the Thompsons feel sorry for the girl. They dismiss the subject lightly with the remark that with such an approach to life, it is no wonder that Third World countries do not develop!

Grace has been quite impressed by all the material accoutrements and mechanical, electric and electronic gadgets and appliances at the Thompsons'. In Zambia, as well as in other Third World countries, such items are the trimmings and trappings of wealth, status, and power. In terms of family structure, however, Grace thinks it is strange, if not downright unfeeling and irresponsible, that the Thompsons say they would not have Mr. Thompson's elderly mother live with them. To Grace, it is surprising that the Thompsons do not seem to understand or appreciate her sense of affection, loyalty, and obligation to her elders. The Thompsons do not only seem to discuss members of their own extended families detachedly and dispassionately, they also act as if they are quite removed and uninvolved with them. It is rather incomprehensible to Grace that the "rich" Thompsons would have cousins who are "poor" and jobless, and that the Thompsons would talk about it openly as if it is not unusual. What seems worse to Grace is that the Thompsons do not care and are not embarrassed about the situation, nor do they act involved and proud of a cousin who has an influential position in the federal government. However, the most baffling thing to Grace is what she considers the shameless discarding of Ed Thompson's mother in a nursing home.

Individual orientation toward one's role and position in life is, by and large, a function of the societal environment in which one is reared. A person's expectations, aspirations, and obligations in a society where the nuclear family is the basic unit are different from their counterparts' expectations in societies centered on the extended family, tribe, or clan.

In the United States, where the nuclear family is the basic unit, children are reared with an emphasis on independence (Hsu 1963). From their early years, children are taught and are expected to learn to develop self-reliance. Children and parents grow up looking forward to the day when the children leave the house and live on their own. The children look forward to their independence and freedom from parental authority, and the parents look forward to their independence and freedom from filial obligations. It is a continuing, incessant process of orientation toward the future. Children and parents expect the future to provide them with the opportunity for freedom from each other. Each side is continually preparing plans for things to do and places to go alone or with their peers in the future. Nowhere in that process does either side envision or expect the family to continue to live together for life except as a misfortune. Children grow up with the belief that one's obligations are to oneself and one's immediate family. The child learns that the family is composed of a father, a mother, their children, and to varying degrees (depending on geography, ethnic background, and parental status consciousness) perhaps grandparents, uncles, aunts, and their children. Primarily, however, everyone plans for the future and old age, and everyone's responsibility is to oneself and one's spouse and children.

In societies centered on the extended family, tribe, or clan, children are raised in an atmosphere of mutual dependence and intense interpersonal relationships. Children grow up in environments that value, honor, and venerate old age. Early in life people develop a heightened sense of awareness of their roles and obligations in the cycles of families and friends around them. The families are close and large, and the members are quite involved in each other's lives. In such societies, it is rather difficult to enumerate who the members of a family are. This writer recalls a time when as a child in a primary school class in Egypt, his young North American teacher asked him to list the members of his family, and he could not do it. Every time he would arrive at a number, he would remember another uncle or aunt or cousin. When he went home, he asked his mother the same question and felt better later when no one in the house could decide on a figure. Every time a member in the house decided to close the count, another uncle or aunt brought up the names in another household and everybody agreed that they certainly were part of the family—then mother or grandmother would go into explaining the genealogy.

Children grow up in these types of societies with a strongly embedded sense of obligation to the large, surrounding family and with an orientation toward the past and its traditions for guidance and behavior. In rural as well as in urban areas, a family's main investment is in its children and close relatives, whether by blood, marriage, or frequent inter-action. The old raise, elevate, and try to educate the young, who later on mature, become responsible, and take care of their old. The intense involvement and interpersonal nature of relationships between the gener-ations during all stages of life reinforces the individual's sense of emo-tional, psychological, and economic interdependence, obligations, and expectations from the family, tribe, or clan in the society. Societal func-tions that are impersonal and institutionalized in the United States such as life insurance, medical insurance, day care centers, and nursing homes, and the like, are not only highly personal in traditionally oriented societies but are attended to and performed by members of the immedi-ate household, extended family, or clan as part of one's expectations and obligations in life.

It is no wonder, therefore, that Grace Sibanda is surprised that Helen and Edward Thompson allow Edward's mother to live in a nursing home and feel no shame about it. On the other hand, from the Thompsons' perspective, they think Grace and her fiancé, for all their education, have not been able to develop a sense of independence strong enough to desire a home and a life of their own.

PATTERNS IN HIGH- AND LOW-CONTEXT CULTURES

In the three situations presented and discussed in this paper, com-munication involving members from what Hall (1976) describes as "high- and low-context cultures" ends in frustration and misunderstanding. From the cultural perspective of each participant, his or her behavior and actions are meaningful and rational. Communication breaks down, how-ever, because in every case, the individuals are trying to construe mean-ing from an examination of sets of behavior and their component isolates without trying to understand the intangible, cultural patterns that under-lie and tie the observable behavioral sets (Hall 1959). In each of the three intercultural situations, the participants judge and condemn each other's nonverbal behavior without familiarity with the behavior's historical, so-cial, and cultural context.

Hall has contrasted the two types of cultures as "high" and "low" context. In high-context cultures people are intensely aware of each other and greatly involved with each other, while in low-context cul-tures relationships between people and their expectations of each other are less intense and are governed by rather clearly defined rules. People's patterns of communicative behavior in high-context cultures are not usually spelled out. A lot of the ongoing exchanged messages in such cultures are preprogrammed and internalized in the people's minds. The programming process is related to the emotional, psychological, and physical proximity in which members of high-context cultures are reared, in both rural or urban homes. The intense interpersonal relationships and one's heightened awareness of mutual dependence on one's household, extended family, tribe, or clan are important factors in that process. Consequently,

> a high-context (HC) communication or message is one in which most of the information is either in the physical context or internalized in the person, while very little is in the coded, explicit, transmitted part of the message. A low-context (LC) communication is just the opposite; i.e., the mass of the information is vested in the explicit code. Although no culture exists exclusively at one end of the scale, some are high while others are low. American culture, while not on the bottom, is toward the low end of the scale. (Hall 1976 : 91)

The three intercultural transactions presented in this paper reflect communication between people from high-context and low-context cultures. In every situation, both sides consider a detached behavioral set and try to interpret its isolates rather than study the set in relation and combination with other sets so that the underlying behavior patterns can be established. The results are misunderstanding and frustration.

In reference to the Ford's gift, Mike and Mona Kalb's behavior seems strange and baffling to North American observers. In the high-context cultures of the Middle East, however, guest-host relationships are part and parcel of a complex pattern of hospitality (Yousef 1974). Transactions continuously reflect one's position in the societal, vertical hierarchies. In the Middle East, people relate to each other and conduct their social, business, and political affairs in terms of guest-host relationships with high premiums placed on largesse, friendship, and face-saving (Yousef and Briggs 1975). Thus, in taking away the gift and not commenting on it to the Fords in front of others, the Kalbs, according to their cultural norms, are being tactful and considerate of the feelings of their guests. On the other hand, from the Fords' American, low-context, cultural perspective, behavior in such situations is spelled out. One should receive the gift with an expression of mild surprise, read the accompanying card and feel touched, then open the gift and express ecstacy. The steps are defined and taught, and a breach of any of them is improper and crude.

In the case of Marsha Johnson and Juan Lopez, the North American girl feels disturbed that her fiancé withholds public manifestations of affection from her and deems them improper, while his transactions with his male Latin, Middle Eastern, and southern European friends are sprinkled with lots of touching. To Juan and his friends, however, who were raised in high-context cultures, their behavior is meaningful and congruent. Societal relationships in Latin America, the Middle East, and southern Europe are governed by patterns of honor and shame that are centered on the purity of the sexual behavior and reputations of the females in the family, the tribe, or the clan. [Males in these societies jealously guard their honor through the protection and control of the sexual behavior of their females. Often enough, a woman's sexual indiscretions could result in her demise.[1] By the same token, women in these cultures expect their men to be jealous and protective. A woman would feel deprived, undesirable, and rejected if she did not feel, or could not claim, male protection and jealousy of her honor.]

At present with the spread of urbanization, coeducation, and female participation in businesses and professions, many tabooed male-female interactions are drained of their sexual connotations and are gaining in social acceptability. Social behavior, though, in terms of honor and shame, is still governed to a large extent by female sexual behavior. To Juan his protective behavior and concern for his future wife is thus quite proper and masculine. At the same time, to Marsha the pattern of honor and shame and its nuances that Juan and his friends seem to have in their heads seem too complicated and far-fetched. From her United States low-context, cultural perspective, "good" girls indulge in certain come-on and push-off behaviors, in terms of courtship communication until they get engaged and married and move to the subsequent stages.

The Thompsons' intercultural transaction with Grace Sibanda leaves them surprised and baffled. Grace's seeming lack of interest in independence and having a home and life of her own with her husband, away from their extended family, borders on the pathologic from Helen and Edward's North American perspective. However, Grace, who grew up in a high-context culture, cannot envision or appreciate the notions of individual and nuclear family independence that the Thompsons seem to admire. Grace's response is based on a societal pattern of mutual dependence with which she grew up. In the pattern, members of a household are bound for life in cycles of expectations and obligations to each other and to their extended families, friends, tribes, and clans. The old rear the young who grow up to take care of their old in a sort of a familial welfare system. The old give their all to the upbringing, elevation, and education of their young, who later on, in turn, take pride in supporting and attending to the needs of the old. The pattern also endows age with status and a measure of saintliness, so that hallucinating senility is often considered a state of rapport with the deity. Thus, to

Grace, the idea of nursing homes where the old are supposed to live together and be happy together seems cruel and alien. On the other hand, the Thompsons' upbringing in the North American, low-context culture emphasized a different pattern of independence. From early age, children are encouraged and expected to make their own decisions. The individual grows up with an understanding that his or her own duties and obligations are mainly to oneself and one's immediate family. Independence of one's biological or adoptive family thus becomes an early goal in one's life. Hence, the Thompsons' and Grace's inability to understand each other.

CONCLUSION

The different patterns underlying the intercultural transactions discussed in this paper differ from each other primarily because of the different cultural frames of reference of the participants—those of high-context and low-context. High-context cultures reflect patterns and value systems of people intensely involved in each other's lives, while in low-context cultures relationships are usually looser and less binding. High-context cultures are also marked by behavioral patterns of interdependence, while low-context cultures emphasize independence.

In the intercultural transactions in the situations presented in this paper, breakdowns in communication occur because the individuals try to derive meaning from abstracted behavioral sets rather than from studying the structure of underlying patterns and their meaning in related behavioral sets in related contexts.

NOTES

1. In a report that appeared in the Orange County edition of the *Los Angeles Times*, on July 9, 1973, the following news item was published:

ITALIAN SLAYS HIS BRIDE TO SAVE "HONOR"

FROSINONE, Italy (UPI)—This is 21-year-old Anna Nenna's love story and it is a short one. It began with flowers and rice and ended four days later with her death and her bridegroom's confession of murder.

Police said Salvatore Nappo, 28, told them honor was the reason he drove Anna to a wooded country lane Friday on the fourth day of their honeymoon to put four bullets into her chest.

"I did it for my honor. She was not a virgin and did not have the courage to tell me that," police quoted Nappo as saying.

Nappo, said the doctors, had been mistaken. Anna was a virgin.

REFERENCES

Condon, J. C., and F. S. Yousef, 1975. *An Introduction to Intercultural Communication* (Indianapolis: Bobbs-Merrill).

Hall, E. T., 1959. *The Silent Language* (Greenwich, Conn.: Fawcett).

———, 1977. *Beyond Culture* (Garden City, N.Y.: Anchor).

Hsu, F., 1963. *Clan, Caste, and Club* (New York: Van Nostrand).

Peristiany, J. G., ed., 1965. *Honour and Shame: The Values of the Mediterranean* (London: Weiderfeld and Nicolson).

Shouby, E., 1951. The Influence of the Arabic Language on the Psychology of the Arabs. *Middle East Journal* 5 : 284–302.

Yousef, F. S., 1968. Cross-Cultural Testing: An Aspect of the Resistance Reaction. *Language Learning* 18 (3–4) : 227–234.

———, 1974. Cross-Cultural Communication: Aspects of Contrastive Social Values between North Americans and Middle Easterners. *Human Organization* 33 : 383–387.

———, 1976. Nonverbal Behavior: Some Intricate and Diverse Dimensions in Intercultural Communication. In *Intercultural Communication: A Reader*, Larry A. Samovar and Richard E. Porter, eds. (Belmont, Cal.: Wadsworth), pp. 230–235.

Yousef, F. S., and N. E. Briggs, 1975. The Multinational Business Organization: A Schema for the Training of Overseas Personnel in Communication. In *International and Intercultural Communication Annual*, Vol. II (Falls Church, Va.: Speech Communication Association), pp. 74–85.

The Case of the Disappearing Ethnics

M. ESTELLIE SMITH

Occasionally the field worker is blessed with the opportunity to observe an event or series of events in the community under study that not only encapsulates a variety of sociocultural behaviors and factors but also demands the rethinking of some cherished "truths." Such truths may be fundamental to the ethnographic ordering of the data or to broader analytical concepts. The following study is, first, the account of such an event and, second, a statement of my analysis and the resulting reformulation of hitherto accepted axioms.

PROLOGUE

Texton[1] is a New England industrial town of approximately 100,000 people. Formerly a prosperous nineteenth-century textile center, it has declined in both population and income during the last half-century. Today it is estimated that between 30 and 70 percent of the population are descended from or are newly arrived Portuguese immigrants.[2] Beginning about the 1870's mill owners recruited Portuguese labor, since early contacts with them as fisherfolk, whalers, and agricultural workers had given rise to the stereotype of a hardworking and undemanding people; that is, they were known for being willing to work long hours, under appalling conditions, for low pay, and with little complaining.

Most of the Portuguese were from the mid-Atlantic islands—the Azores, Madeira, and Cape Verde group—and were probably among the most impoverished, isolated, plantation-dominated, small-scale peasants in Europe. Given the chance to escape these overpopulated islands, they began an immigration flow that continued up to the economic catastrophe of the 1930's, though entry into the United States had begun to slow following the Immigration Literacy Law of 1917. Though minimal in its definition of literacy (the mere ability to write one's name made one competent in that skill), the law presented a barrier for the Island Portuguese who, in the first decade of the twentieth century, had the highest illiteracy rate of any American immigrant segment—68.2 percent (Bannick 1917:39–40).[3]

Further restrictive laws, the declining labor market in New England, depressions, and the global war of the 1940's caused the forty-year period between 1920 and 1960 to show a total entry of Portuguese only slightly over 60,000—with almost 20,000 of that figure entering in the year 1921 alone. One may compare this with the period 1881–1920 when over 200,000 entered (Adler 1972:17). Because many of the 60,000 entering after 1920 went to California, the influx of Portuguese into New England slowed to a mere few hundred a year—and this influx was balanced by an almost equal number who emigrated back to Portugal.[4]

Following World War II the rising expectations of minorities and the resulting "radical" agitation led to sociocultural reformulations in various segments of the American populace. This, in turn, led to various changes in the immigration laws. Following the first of these, the Immigration Act of 1965 (75 Stat. 911), Portuguese immigration took a dramatic jump upward. In the period 1961–70 entries exceeded by almost 25 percent the accumulated total for the preceding forty years (1921–60 = 60,334; 1961–70 = 76,064), with approximately 50 percent of that total per year going to the Commonwealth of Massachusetts and, perhaps, another 10 percent going to the neighboring state of Rhode Island.[5] Between the years 1967–69, 41,012 entered the United States with over 18,000 going to Massachusetts—and a majority of these going to the metropolitan Texton area. This happened despite the fact that in that city's textile industry alone the number of jobs in the male labor market between 1950 and 1970 declined from 9,084 to 4,108—a decrease of 54.8 percent (Keerock Rook Associates 1972:21).

This flood of unskilled, primarily rural Portuguese to an area where unemployment was high and where there was a tradition of hostility to Portuguese speakers exacerbated existing relations between the latter and other ethnically defined but basically economically oriented interest groups in the area. A plethora of "Dumb Portygee" jokes saturated the city (e.g., Question: "Why wasn't Christ born in Portugal?" Answer: "Because they couldn't find three wise men" or "Because they couldn't find a virgin"). The city schools were, during a brief period in 1968, channeling one thousand newly arrived Portuguese-speaking children through the school system per month! Ethnic sneers became more overt among the three major categories of non-Portuguese in the town—the descendants of French-Canadian, Irish, and generalized north Europeans. Depending on various factors, one could be told that the Portygees (itself a derogatory term) were "dumb," "disease-ridden" (most commonly, either tubercular or carriers of venereal diseases), "over-sexed," or "left-handed niggers"[6]—to mention only a few allegations.

THE EPISODE

By the early 1970's certain members of the community, for reasons I will explore later, decided that some public steps would have to be taken to mend the increasingly dysfunctional schisms that marked relations between various segments of Texton—schisms based on class, ethnic, and religious differences. As one public official said to me, "This town will just keep going down-hill if we don't start pulling together and cut out this in-fighting." The mayor formed a committee to study the question and suggest ways to improve community relations. Or at the advice of this group, it was decided to go "to the root" of the generalized dissonance. He proclaimed Portuguese Day, which would feature a number of activities emphasizing the positive role that the target group had played in the history of the city. Schools, for instance, were to give special assemblies; the mass media would have commentary and news highlights; businessmen would run ads addressed to or simply congratulating their Portuguese clientele; and the local community college campus would serve as the focal point for an all-day program of exhibits and speakers "familiarizing the community with the contributions of the Portuguese to [Texton]."

The latter was, of course, the main event. A series of speakers representing various walks of life made short speeches throughout the program, which also included music, dancing, and dramatic presentations by immigrant school children. All the speeches concerned the history, esthetic contributions, and desirable stereotypic traits of the Portuguese (such as "their natural love of beauty"). Several of the most recent immigrants were included on the program and those who introduced them stressed that such individuals were proof that, "in this land of opportunity" those who worked diligently would "fulfill the American dream." The last speaker stated: "The Portuguese are good neighbors. We have seen that they are loyal, hard-working, diligent, and have an eye to the future. They are industrious, God-fearing, and law-abiding. They courageously came here to start a new life and they have succeeded. Americans can learn an important lesson from them." A spirit of bonhomie seemed to pervade the city and one local TV station, in summarizing events on the late evening news, assured its viewers that, "understanding and good-fellwship has marked this day, a day that won't be forgotten soon, a day that marks the beginning of a new era in our city."

AFTERMATH

By the next day, local radio talk shows received calls from individuals identifying themselves as "Americans" (and even "real" or "loyal" Americans) who wished to comment on Portuguese Day. The majority of remarks were hostile, even bitter and, more importantly, some of the most acrimonious speeches came from those who began or ended their comments with phrases such as, "I'm of Portuguese descent. . . ." Since many of these calls were made to a local Portuguese language station the sneers and ridicule directed toward the laudatory aura of the celebration quickly generated angry counter-callers and soon insults were being flung back and forth. Less than forty-eight hours later the editorial page of the local newspaper also became an arena for the feud.

And feud it obviously was. Portuguese were charging Portuguese with being "rotten Americans," "lazy," "jealous," "money-hungry," "cut-throat towards their own," "scabs," and "scroungers." Non-Portuguese publically stayed aloof but, in private, would typically shrug and say, "What else would you expect?" or "They're always knifing each other." It soon became clear that the lines of cleavage were between those Portuguese who were native born or had come to this country before World War II and those who had arrived in the post-1960 era. But, while the demarcation was obvious, and the claims for why such a split existed were all too explicit, what was not clear were the processes that had created the division. This attempt at interethnic communication had not only failed to increase understanding, worse, it had led to behavior on the part of the Portuguese-Americans that had reinforced the negative stereotype which non-Portuguese had—and which the latter could now claim the Portuguese themselves had confirmed and validated.

ETHNOGRAPHIC ANALYSIS

It should be emphasized that the major concern of the mayor and his commission was the creation of some event that would generate a spirit of good will and fellowship—something that would spark a new spirit in a town trying to overcome its history in recent years of dismal decline and current apathy. The town leaders need not have focused on the Portuguese but could, in fact, have stressed some other theme—say, Texton's industrial history, which showed that it had been able to survive the loss of textile production, its bankruptcy and economic difficulties, and to an extent to fight back by substituting a thriving garment industry. Such an alternative might have been expected since, up to this point, the Portuguese-Americans had been little noted by non-Portuguese save as factory fodder and as a negative force in certain of the town's affairs. As one non-Portuguese put it:

> the town needed a pep talk and the Portygees seemed the best target. I frankly wouldn't care if they all got the hell out. But we need to get the town moving and, with the TV and everything talking about "bilingualism" and "biculturalism" and "cultural pluralism" and all that, this seemed the best approach. It seemed like a good idea at the time. How did we know what a hornet's nest we'd stir up?

Thus, it was the larger society's emphasis on the betterment of minority relations, coupled with the dramatic influx of new Portuguese immigrants, that led to the selection of the particular strategy of Portuguese Day.

Unfortunately language, as has long been recognized, can and usually does communicate a multiplicity of messages. This is all to the good if we consider how complicated the system would be otherwise. It also presents problems; in this case each segment of the town received the same message differently. For one thing, there were really two groups of Portuguese-Americans.

In discussing the message of Portuguese Day, Portuguese-American informants themselves defined two groups—as I have already indicated. Each informant, regardless of the group to which he perceived himself as belonging, identified one category as containing those early arrivals who considered themselves (and were considered by recent immigrants) as Americans. Standing in contrast to this group were those Portuguese who had arrived in the post-1950 period. All Portuguese-Americans classified these individuals as Portuguese. Although at other times in my fieldwork these categories shifted or overlapped in content, during the investigatory period of two months following the events of Portuguese Day, informants relied solely on the temporal criterion for the categorization of an individual.

These two segments and the non-Portuguese population received three different messages from the events of Portuguese Day. The public message, the message that non-Portuguese had intended to communicate and themselves received was, in summary: "We value the contribution which, since the early days of Texton, all those of you who came from Portugal have made. Let's forget the past and work together for a better future. Here is our hand in friendship."

The message received by the early immigrants (whom I call "The Old Portuguese" and who, in this context, considered themselves Americans) was: "You Americans of Portuguese descent have never amounted to much and we've always let you know it. If you had behaved as these new immigrants have when you and your ancestors arrived in this country, we would have respected you and recognized your place in the community by honoring *you* with a Portuguese Day."

The message that the "New Portuguese"—the post-1960 immigrants—received was: "Right on, friends! You're out there being successful at the only thing that brings anyone to this country—making money. We may not like you but, at least, you're not like those dumb forerunners of your group who tried to be the mythical 'Good Americans' in that phoney melting pot that the school books tried to fool everybody with."

The Old Portuguese rejected the implication that they were part of that community of Portuguese about whom such admiring remarks were made because, for many years, they had been told that being Portuguese was bad. They had had it drummed into them—in schools, in church, on the job, by the media, by their non-Portuguese neighbors—that the only good immigrant was a good American. And, by God!, that's what they had tried to be—that's what they *were*. They were not Portuguese! Thus, they were distressed and embittered by the message of Portuguese Day because they perceived that the same ethnicity that had worked against them and, especially in their first years in this country, had made their lives so difficult, was now A Good Thing. It was being used by the new arrivals to gain economic privileges ranging from cheap school lunches and on-the-job training stipends to college scholarships and funded-research positions with a bicultural genesis that "everyone knew were cream-puff jobs."

The New Portuguese, on the other hand, knew without doubt that they were Portuguese—they had been born in Portugal, Portuguese was their native language. And they were certainly not Americans simply because they were here; they had immigrated here but next year they might emigrate to Canada, or Brazil, or anywhere—even back home. Obviously, simply working in a country doesn't make you part of that citizenry. Equally obvious was "the fact" that they were "The Portuguese" who were being addressed—the ones from whom Americans could learn a lesson.

Clearly, Portuguese Day did not create the disjuncture between Old and New Portuguese. That existed prior to the event, which merely made the differentiation explicit. What had inhibited the bonding mechanism and created the schism?

I would suggest that at least three factors were at work: (*a*) a competition for scarce resources in a depressed economy; (*b*) a higher level of expectations in the newly arrived immigrant group; (*c*) a monetary base for corporateness among the latter that was not available to earlier arrivals.

The New Portuguese, because of their unskilled labor status, the language barrier, and the usual occupational channeling processes, initially sought employment in the same sectors where Americans of Portuguese descent were already working—albeit intermittently, at low pay, and in a labor-glutted market. Thus, it wasn't long before charges were made that New Portuguese who got jobs in the traditional employment sectors were excluding an American from employment.

Increasing numbers of Old Portuguese argued that it was necessary to erect employment barriers to protect themselves (even though it was understood that an immigrant who could not get employment might "disgrace the good name of the Portuguese"—as well as possibly add to the tax burden). They resented it when such barriers were surmounted; many of them remembered the struggles they had gone through and believed the new immigrants did not appreciate how much easier life is in the present day. "They brag about how much faster they get richer than us and say it's because they're smarter, better workers. They don't see how they're getting benefits we never got. It's not like it was in the old days."

The New Portuguese, better educated and more knowledgeable about the world due to Portugal's inevitable modernization, were more capable of devising and shifting to alternate economic strategies when they saw how minimal were the opportunities in the traditional employment areas. They began to create new income sources and this was, in large measure, aided by an easier credit potential as well as higher income than "in the old days." By borrowing, pooling resources, working at jobs that often came from under-the-counter deals with bosses, floor supervisors, and union representatives, a significant number of them were soon able to accumulate sufficient seed money to open small businesses, buy rental property, and finance other entrepreneurial activities.

In short, the Old Portuguese were successful not so much in keeping out competitive labor as in forcing the new arrivals to explore other avenues. The initial success of these latecomers encouraged even more immigrants to leave Portugal, thus adding to the excess labor pool and depressing (in absolute terms) the local economy still further. Simultaneously, however, the continuing influx of immigrants actually generated an increased demand for those entrepreneurs who had initiated services such as ethnic food stores, driving schools, ethnic restaurants, and immigrant aid services—all directed to the needs of immigrants. Further, continuing immigration created a housing shortage and this led to increased rental income from those same tenements the early New

Portuguese had bought cheaply.[7] Thus, though adding to the overall economic problems of Texton, the immigrants created a selective prosperity for some of the populace.[8]

The second factor, that of higher expectations, is equally important. Those same forces that were to produce a revolution in Portugal had also changed attitudes among those who immigrated. Despite their having generally the same rural background, the New Portuguese do not come to this country as uneducated and naive as those who arrived prior to World War II. This, coupled with their arrival at a time when attitudes in this country concerning immigrants, ethnics, and minorities are undergoing at least superficial change, has created a more favorable milieu for those who wish to become rich and successful. For one thing, it allows them to do so far more rapidly and spectacularly than was (and still is) possible for the Old Portuguese. The latter, far more consistently, have had such successes denied them.

The Old Portuguese can, on the whole, rationalize this "success" in only one way. They reject the explanation that the New Portuguese offer—that early arrivals have failed because they are lazy, servile, and lacking incentive. They argue that the newcomers—the Greenhorns or Greenies—are "ignorant" (used by the Old Portuguese to mean unmannerly, rude, uncouth, brash, and aggressive), "money-hungry," "slumlords," "grasping," "scheming," "cheats and liars," "exploiters of their own kind," and worst of all, "willing to live like peasants do in the Old Country—like animals—just to get rich quick."

The attitude of the New Portuguese to such charges can be summed up by the following comments from a former landlord of mine:

> For years America was like a chamber pot. Like it says on the Statue of Liberty, "Send us your poor, dumb, and miserable." So we did. We used this country to crap in.
>
> Now times are different and we're different. We're smart and educated. We work hard to get places. The people who come now aren't like those Americans who came over before. Now we're respected. Americans may not like us—that's always the way when you don't do good enough or when you do too good. But they got to admit we can make it like those other people never could, except once in a while a smart one.

BROADER IMPLICATIONS

We have seen that the meaning content of words such as *Portuguese*, *Portuguese-American*, *American*, *we*, and *them* was not the same to all the participants within the message field. It is important to note, however, that because the Portuguese agreed on ethnic boundaries in this specific instance does not mean that the categories are always similarly defined. The lines of segmentation drawn here can, in other contexts, fuse or become more dentritic. The same individual can be American, Portuguese-American, Portuguese, Island Portuguese, Azorean, Michalense, or Ponta Delgadian—a widespread if not even universal process. (The discussions of Nagata, 1974, and Kasfir, 1976, offer similar arguments.) Each of these categories has unique stereotypic characteristics that mark the individual so identified—by choice or imposition—as like his fellows and unlike others. Once the distinction has been made, those who are outside that category stand in a dialectic relationship; behavior predicated on the basis of that identifying process is, for at least some of the actors, some of the time, channeled—not infrequently along the lines of a self-fulfilling prophecy. I must emphasize, however, that categorization can and does shift as the arena shifts.

If boundaries and symbolic markers shift, however, it seems reasonable to argue that a concern with the "reality" or nature of such boundaries and markers per se can (though not necessarily) have a scientifically trivial emphasis. The focus of our analytical concern should be the socioeconomic processes at work in the situation. Ethnicity, like most if not all cultural identities, is primarily a tool that enables humans to identify themselves and others for the purpose of formulating behavior. Homogeneity or diversity is imposed for purposes of categorization; such categorizations then allow prediction and the weighing of the potential outcome of various choices in the decision-making range. After the decision is made, action (even when it takes the form of "nonaction") follows.

It is the drama itself, then, which must be the focus of our attention, not the masks of the dramatis personae. Actors shift statuses and roles, but "the play's the thing." It is the structure and dynamic processes of the drama that are important, not the identities of the actors themselves. As in a football game, it is not the uniforms, the cheerleader's rhymes, the songs, mascots, banners, and other symbolic representations of the contest which grip us—they are merely cues for our responses. It is the game itself, and specifically our own team. The player whose behavior we hissed last year is traded to our team and now, this year, becomes a hero for us.

We are left, then, with the argument that ethnic identity, just as many other identities, has fluid and flexible dimensions, primarily useful only in terms of a situational analysis. Identity is the overt manifestation of symbols, symbols which are only suprasegmental markers for and in a human dialogue. It is the dynamics of the dialogue—the responses generated rather than the words themselves—that should draw our attention.

Along these lines Shaibutani and Kwan (1965:208) have suggested that "the degree to which consciousness of kind develops among people varies with consistency of differential treatment." I would propose that the more heterogeneous a society and the greater the potential or actual contact among members of that society, the greater the variety of "consistent treatments." Somewhat paradoxically, the more heterogeneous a society, the larger the number of "consistent" identities which one may have imposed or at his disposal, and the more consistent the possibility of differential treatment in differential spatiotemporal settings. It is knowledge of that differential treatment that creates strategic options, each of which may be evaluated as to its "adaptive" utility in this or that situation.[9]

This brings us to the third factor at work, the potential for corporate group formation, accessible for the New Portuguese but unavailable to the early immigrants. American society beyond Texton's boundaries had decreed that minorities and immigrants were now to be treated differently from their predecessors (however these terms are defined and no matter who is included or excluded.) As post-1960 ethnics, the New Portuguese were given access to resources not available in earlier years—special educational programs, housing and business loans, and the like. Such factors encouraged what Bennett (1975) has called "a coalition for advantage" and the distinction that Despres has drawn between an ethnic group—i.e., a corporate collectivity—and an atomistic ethnic population was able to become a reality within the Portuguese-American community (cf. Despres 1975:195–204). The base for corporateness among the New Portuguese was minority aid funds, those federal, state, and foundation monies that encouraged entrepreneurial and managerial individuals to form organizations through which access to those funds (and jobs and power) could be gained. Such organizations then served as a real and symbolic locus for a coalition or coalitions which, as Despres itemizes them, "possess a unitary set of external relations, a relatively exclusive body of common affairs, and procedures which are more or less adequate to the administration of these affairs" (1975:196). Thus, forces at work in the macrosystem led to an alteration in the microsystem—which fed back into other subsystems as well as, ultimately, the macrosystem—all of which were altered. Economic and political factors led to the creation of corporate entities to meet the macrosystemic expectations and exploit these new resources. The resultant corporate groups became symbolic entities with which even traditionally tracked New Portuguese (who were not directly involved) could vicariously identify. The society beyond Texton provided a new mode of "consistent differential treatment" and thereby provided the base for the crystallization of a corporate group, where only an ethnic population had formerly existed. In the process, however, it helped to generate internal segmentation, creating a more narrowly defined population than the non-Portuguese of Texton knew.[10]

I have previously stated that talk of boundaries is scientifically trivial unless it is clear that such boundaries are unstable and situationally defined. Such suprastructure detracts from the enduring processes that are repetitively played out in arena after arena no matter how the setting and the actors stylistically vary or are symbolically identified. This needs reiterating, for since the work of Barth (1969), more stress has been placed on the structural implications of the boundaries than on the processes that both create and are affected by that structure. This is strange, for even Barth (1969 : 13), like Weber and others since Weber, stresses that first and foremost ethnic groups are human collectivities based on an assumption of common origin. The question that must concern us is: "What is the process by which this assumption is born?" We might, for example, begin by stressing the inverse proposition and seek to find the operational principles of noncommonality—i.e., how and for what reasons are outsiders and nonmembers identified and excluded?

I have suggested that, though perhaps primitive, it seems fruitful to hypothesize that the critical components in the categorizing process are situational and pragmatic. (Nagata, 1974, has an excellent statement on this.) Identity components are part of the "communication of transactions," and combinatorially are as ephemeral or durable as the transaction. Even the most pristine of ethnics, for example (are there any such?), will find his identity extended or delimited by other components such as religion (WASP), language (speaker of Standard American English), region (southerner), or phenotype (again, WASP). This perspective argues that one limns out identity markers in order to define the expected parameters in a transaction. We all as humans must communicate with other humans; identities serve as the basis for that communication, for interaction and dialogue. If, however, we were forced to make idio-identifications each time we interacted with someone, the margin of error would be increased and individual stress would grow to intolerable limits because of the high complexity of situational variables.

It is time to recognize that the essentially normalizing nature of culture is a stereotyping process—one which conditions us to ignore or emphasize the situational components of events, after which we perform the "appropriate" behavior. Such stereotyping has the short-term positive function of reducing stress and, ideally, of facilitating communication. It also has the potential for a dysfunctional simplification, one that becomes increasingly dysfunctional to the extent that our assessment is disconsonant with that of others in the set—when it is incorrect, inappropriate, inadequately refined, situationally monolithic, or when repressive goals underlie the basis of the stereotype that structures the interaction.

In conclusion, one of the lessons that the anecdote from Texton offers is that it demonstrates the great potential for dissonance—using this term as both conflict and communication theorists apply it—that lies in those situations where the actors believe they have a code in common but do not, when they believe they have a nexus of common understanding which, in fact, does not exist. We must accept that understanding can never be absolute because no two people or groups ever experience the same cultural history and to the extent that they have not, to that extent will all communication be so meaning-full that it contains non-equivalent messages. Thus, the more culturally heterogeneous a population is, the greater the possibility that the message will gain in ambiguity and dissonance potential. This should serve as notice that a critical need in message sending is redundancy—sending the so-called same message many times (cf. Murray Leaf's comments on this, 1976: 4–5). The extension of this is, of course, that we must not only strive to be consistent in the messages we send, we must also learn to listen to the responses, for they tell us what was actually heard—what the receiver(s) understood us to say.

Interethnic communication is concerned with the group dynamics of message sending—a situation that, in the final analysis, is only quantitatively different from interpersonal communication. This has the frightening implication that the capacity for a breakdown in communication increases exponentially with the size of the participating population. Conversely, it also implies that the capacity for a significant dialogue may also increase exponentially. Let us hope that the growing concern with and recognition of the monumental difficulties involved in interethnic communication will help achieve a genuine dialogue before the dissonance overwhelms us.

NOTES

1. Texton is a pseudonym. See Smith (1975) for a broader discussion of this city.
2. An accurate figure is difficult to present since (*a*) names have been an-

glicized, (*b*) intermarriage of ethnics offers an identity choice for offspring, (*c*) many individuals reject their Portuguese ancestry because of the low status of Portuguese in this area.

3. There were forty-one ethnic categories listed, ranging from "African" to "West Indian" and including "Other peoples" and "not specified." In second- and third-ranking positions, respectively, were the Turks (59.5 percent) and Mexicans (57.2 percent) (Bannick 1916 : 39–40).

4. The first quota law of 1921 restricted national immigration to the equivalent of 3 percent of their countrymen who had been in the U.S. in 1910; the second quota law of 1924 shifted the base figure to that of the American population in 1890; and the third revision of the National Origins Law (1929) decreed that the number of each nationality admitted per year was "to bear the same ratio to the total quota of 150,000 as the number of that national origin in the US in 1920 bore to the total population then" (Novotny 1971 : 130).

5. Massachusetts has begun to keep figures on such immigrants but Rhode Island has not.

6. This refers to the fact that the Portuguese-speaking Cape Verdeans are African Blacks, giving rise to the belief that all Portuguese are to a greater or lesser degree black. As one Irish-American informant put it, "A nigger's a nigger, no matter how white they look. And I don't want any of them— Portygee or whatever—in my house, in my neighborhood, or in my kid's schools. And they goddamn well better keep to their own churches too!"

7. One typical example is provided by Mr. X who, within a year of his arrival, bought a three-story, six-apartment tenement (a term which in this region refers only to the style of building), paying $600 down on its $5,500 cost. Rents have remained relatively stable, averaging $70 per month per apartment over the past ten years. He has continued to add to his list of rental homes and now controls four such buildings, which bring him an average income of $1,600 per month. Although everyone is aware that all new immigrants do not buy their own homes, let alone become landlords, the spectacular accomplishments of those who have become successful in this area colors the stereotype of the New Portuguese—positively from their own perspective, negatively from the perspective of others. Out of a sample of 31 immigrants who have rental property, 19 of them owned 4 tenements, 3 owned 3, 5 owned 2, and one each owned 7, 8, 11, and 16. Additionally, 46 other individuals owned a multifamily house or tenement in which they themselves lived. The Old Portuguese point to the people who own several properties and complain, as did one such typical informant, "This, while I'm still paying off the mortgage on the house I live in, with my parents being born in this country!"

8. E.g., the New Portuguese could have become militant or stayed acquiescent (in the manner of earlier immigrants) but they chose instead to adopt an amalgam of the two—militant enough to argue for aid funds on grounds of discrimination as well as encouraging ethnic support of ethnic businesses, professional and educational personnel, but accepting enough of the dumb stereotype so that non-Portuguese were lulled as to the extent of the "threat" they represented. The Dumb Portygee jokes also served as an outlet for the hostility that, inevitably, was surfacing more and more.

9. It is important to note that strategies are only relatively adaptive and

the choice of a strategy (*a*) is never really free but is structured by the range
of choices that are both in fact and cognitively available; (*b*) may, post hoc,
be maladaptive despite the action being selected for its potential as the maxi-
mally adaptive response. Thus, for the Old Portuguese, ethnicity was mini-
mized as a strategy, being signaled publicly to the community only when it
emphasized the traditional arts, crafts, folklore, religious focus, and recrea-
tional aims of the group (e.g., sports clubs, the Holy Ghost Feast, marching
band clubs). The New Portuguese emphasized ethnicity as it identified them
as a deprived and exploited minority group. The non-Portuguese used the
identity not only to exclude the Portuguese from power groups in the occupational, educational, economic, and political sectors (so as to keep control
within their "old-boy" network) but also to channel personnel into least desirable but functionally necessary positions. The extent to which any of these
identifying strategies was, in fact, the maximal adaptive strategy is open to
debate but, unfortunately, we cannot test for it!

10. The Portuguese themselves see many ethnic markers as adaptive,
"masking strategies" used to deceive others. So, for example, a multitude of
Dumb Portygee jokes mushroomed at just the time when the New Portuguese
began to utilize alternate income tracks, especially the federal, state, and
foundation monies discussed.

11. Barth's work is also flawed by variously vague or sweeping generalizations. For example, given the fluidity in time and space that marks most
ethnic populations in America (or anywhere else) we would be hard put to
identify boundaries or membership by using his criterion that, "The organizational feature which . . . *must* be general for *all* interethnic relations is *a
systematic set of rules* governing interethnic social encounters" (Barth 1969:
16; italics mine). How many of us, without forcing the data or our analysis,
could truly demonstrate that such a systematic set of rules governs the interethnic relations with which we are concerned?

REFERENCES

Adler, James P., 1972. *Ethnic Minorities in Cambridge: The Portuguese*
(Cambridge, Mass.: City of Cambridge Printing Department).
Bannick, Christian John, 1916. *Portuguese Immigration to the United States:
Its Distribution and Status* (A.B. thesis, Stanford University. Issued 1971
by R and E Research Associates, San Francisco).
Barth, Fredrik, ed., 1969. *Ethnic Groups and Boundaries: The Social Organ-
ization of Culture Differences* (London: George Allen and Unwin).
Bennett, John W., ed., 1975. *The New Ethnicity: Perspectives from Ethnol-
ogy*. 1973 Proceedings of the American Ethnological Society (St. Paul,
Minn.: West Publishing).
Despres, Leo A., ed., 1975. *Ethnicity and Resources Competition in Plural
Societies* (The Hague: Mouton).
Kasfir, Nelson, 1976. *The Shrinking Political Arena: Participation and Eth-
nicity in African Politics, with a Case Study of Uganda* (Berkeley: Uni-
versity of California Press).

Keerock Rook and Associates, 1972. *The Final Report of the* [Texton] *Community Renewal Program* (Alexander, Me.: Keerock Rook and Associates).

Leaf, Murray J., 1976. Two Directions in Metatheory. Manuscript.

Nagata, Judith, 1974. What is a Malay? Situational Selection of Ethnic Identity in a Plural Society. *American Ethnologist* 1(2) : 331–350.

Novotny, Ann, 1971. *Strangers at the Door: Ellis Island, Castle Garden, and the Great Migration to America* (Riverside, Conn.: Chatham Press).

Shaibutani, Tamotsu, and Kian M. Kwan (with Robert H. Billigmeier), 1965. *Ethnic Stratification: A Comparative Approach* (New York: Macmillan).

Smith, M. Estellie, 1975. A Tale of Two Cities: The Reality of Historical Differences. *Urban Anthropology* 4(1) : 61–72.

Cultural Barriers and Interethnic Communication in a Multiethnic Neighborhood

José M. Molina

In the study of interethnic communication, one place to begin is with the local grass-roots level of neighborhood life as seen in community organization.[1] This chapter is an attempt to delineate some of the dynamics of social group formation and leadership among various ethnic enclaves as viewed by one community organizer.

It is commonly assumed that the community organizer organizes communities. That is not a true assumption. The champion of community organization, Saul Alinsky (1963), says that there is "no such animal" as an unorganized community. Rothstein (1973) states that community organizers organize organizations. What a community organizer does, in essence, is to draw the lines and identify the links already existing in a real or a political community.

By a *real community* I mean a group of people interrelated by common interest or culture, kinship, or friendship, who may but do not necessarily live in the same geographical area. By a *political community* I mean a group of people who live within certain geographical boundaries that have been defined by the political system. The unpretentious role of a community organizer is that of bringing about an interaction among groups of people who are already interrelated in some way—to put into communication and into action an existing community.

Over the past eight years I have been organizing in the Miami area. During that time I have participated in several seminars, and I have observed particular organization patterns which have developed in the United States. It is clear to me that most community organization has followed the already-existing lines of racial or ethnic minorities within the larger American society. From the beginning, I want to point out that these efforts have certainly been effective in solving problems specific to a limited number of organized minorities. They have not, however, proved useful in solving problems common to several minority and majority groups.

The tendency to organize ethnic or racial minorities is based on our history, in which a dominant racial group played the role of oppressor while others fell into the role of oppressed. Slavery and oppression were real, and recent. So real and so fresh are these events and relationships that it is impossible to forget them. For this reason most of the organizing has been done around our history of oppression, with the goal of "liberation" for the minority peoples. In addition, it is obvious that it is easier to organize groups of people who share the same physical characteristics and cultural background than groups with racial and cultural differences. In such cases, people have strong common bonds that are for the organizer easy to identify and to experience. Trust and identification emerge almost spontaneously.

I do not want to undervalue the goals of such minority group organizations. When viewed, however, within the total societal context, it appears that these types of groups have been isolating the oppressed from the overall society, and that by organizing in this way we have promoted antagonism between the organized minorities and the other segments of our pluralistic society, some of which are equally oppressed.

In an example from my own experience, early efforts at organization by the Puerto Rican community of Miami were first opposed by some Chicano, Black, and Cuban leaders who perceived this organization as cutting into their own "slice of the pie." I am very pessimistic, therefore, about any lasting social change through this type of "competitive" organizing.

In recent years newspapers have carried articles with such titles as "Ten Years Later," and there have been congressional reports substantiating the lack of any real social change in living conditions for places like the Los Angeles community of Watts. In these cases the organization of minority groups resulted either in the solution of a specific problem or need that benefited only a segment or a limited number of the oppressed people, or in a temporary solution, and things soon rolled back to the status quo ante. The most common failing is that this system "co-opts"[2] the leadership of the deprived group and creates a new elite who enjoy power, privilege, and prestige; with few exceptions, this new elite forgets about their followers, brothers, and sisters. In addition, when the elite of a deprived group attain power, they themselves frequently suppress the voices and aspirations of their own people and become the new oppressors.

Organizations of poor people often result in social services and programs. The natural outcome of this is that the programs are staffed with members of the organized population, as a means of defining the program's "clientele." I would like to refer at this point, to my own experience in Wynwood, a Dade County neighborhood in the northwest area of Miami. As a community organizer my geographical focus or territory was the Wynwood neighborhood.[3]

Wynwood was never 100 percent Puerto Rican. It was, nevertheless, "home" for a large number in the Puerto Rican community who are dispersed throughout the northwest region of the city. At the time I began working there the majority of these people had very low incomes, were unemployed, or were on welfare. Not a single organization or social program existed in the area. Four years later, in 1972–1973, as a result of an organization composed of Puerto Ricans residing not only in Wynwood but also in adjacent areas, a number of social service programs flourished in the neighborhood.

The new programs had the Puerto Rican "seal of approval," and in some cases the name "Puerto Rican." With few exceptions, they were staffed by Puerto Ricans. All of these programs had a definite flavor of the Puerto Rican culture. While these programs mushroomed in the Wynwood community, however, poor families of other ethnic groups moved into the neighborhood: Black Americans, Latins from all Latin American countries, and Haitian refugees. At the same time many Puerto Ricans were being pushed out toward the neighboring areas to the north. A majority of the Wynwood population, however, remains Puerto Rican.[4]

My experience indicates that Puerto Ricans living outside the Wynwood boundaries (Edison, Little River, public housing in Larchmont Gardens, Opa Locka, Carol City, etc.) have been traveling through intervening territories to go back and forth to Wynwood in order to get social services.[5] Most of them do not have their own transportation, and public transportation is very deficient in these regions. It is also interesting that, although social service programs exist in the areas where they actually live, this "real community" of people prefers to return to the political community that provides them with identity. Meanwhile, in contrast, newcomers to the Wynwood community—non-Puerto Ricans—have been resistant to using the programs that exist in their neighborhood.

I have been on the inside of these programs and very close to the directors and staff. Among all of these people there is a clear consciousness that the programs are funded with government money, and that every poor family living in Wynwood is entitled to these services. Another positive aspect is that almost everyone within the program staff is bilingual, speaking both English and Spanish. In spite of this positive attitude of the staff and their ability to communicate, the new residents of Wynwood have made relatively little use of their services. Even other Spanish-speaking groups, Latin and Haitian groups in which I have been involved in the neighborhood, have expressed to me their desire to have "their own programs."

Gradually, however, this situation is beginning to change, and the staffs are being integrated to include Cubans, Central and South Americans, Dominicans, Blacks, and Haitians. Other factors helping non-Puerto Rican residents of Wynwood to utilize their neighborhood services are the openness and insistence of the program directors to serve everybody and their efforts to encourage non-Puerto Rican organizations to instill in their members a sense of identity with neighborhood services. Still, the majority of the consumers are Puerto Rican.

Both facts—the traveling of the "outside" Puerto Ricans to the area, and the passive resistance of the non-Puerto Ricans living in the area—show that the delivery of social services is greatly affected by subcultural control of the programs. My experience indicates that the name of the organization, the main spoken language, the race and color of the staff, and the cultural flavor of the agency in large measure draw the boundaries and define the clientele.

As a breath of fresh air blowing throughout the organizational field, a new trend is now in motion in this country—in San Francisco, Los Angeles, Cleveland, Arkansas, North Carolina, Connecticut, and elsewhere. I am referring to multiethnic, multiracial, majority constituency organizations. Mike Miller (1974) writes: "Americans of all kinds and color are organizing to take back power of government that is constitutionally theirs. A new brand of democratic populism is developing in the cities with newly emerging leaders at its head." Bert De Leeuw (1974) spells out the new organizational trend in energetic words: "New organizations are being built that extend beyond the boundaries and interests of specific neighborhoods (and groups) and engage broad bases of people in action around broad issues of social and economic justice."

Wynwood is actually a neighborhood that is physically integrated. In July 1975 we launched the first efforts of organizing the Wynwood community along the lines of the new organizational trend, that is, a neighborhood organization of multiethnic and multiinterest composition, which in a later stage will be part of a broad coalition. I wish to share my experience in this effort, as an example of the new organizational trend.

In forming the new style of organization, our first step was to use workers and organizers whose backgrounds reflected the several ethnic groups that compose Wynwood. I have observed that people respond most readily to an invitation to organize if it is given by an organizer from their own race or ethnic group. In other words, in a practical sense the race of the organizer determines in great part the ethnic or racial makeup of the organization of that block or street.

Another of the early steps in our organization process was to have a "house meeting." Depending on the background of the house owner— Haitian, Cuban, or Puerto Rican—the majority of those in attendance tended also to be Haitian, Cuban, or Puerto Rican. The result of this fact was that, regardless of the physical integration of the block and the multiethnic approach in the mind of the organizer, the race or ethnic group of the host of the first house meetings defined the dominant racial factor, tending to create a small racial group rather than an integrated block club. This experience supports the research findings of Gerlach and Hine on social movements (1970), in which they show that recruitment into grass-roots-level organizations occurs through preexisting social networks of relatives and friends, not through geographical proximity.

The key to making the new model work is to disover issues that transcend cultural barriers and local interest and that appeal to the self-interests of the diverse groups involved in order to build a majority constituency organization. In attempting this, however, we have been encountering a big obstacle. Although we are able to discover problems that are common to all target groups, different ethnic values and experiences result in seemingly incompatible ideas about methods of solving them. Some ethnic groups have developed a genius for advocacy or radical confrontation, some like to work within the system and appeal to human authority, and others prefer low-profile "do-it-yourself" methods. Still others believe in the efficacy of prayer.

Let me illustrate this situation. One of the problems that appeared to be common to everybody in Wynwood was crime, that is, robberies, breaks-ins, assaults. The issue emerged constantly in conversations with individuals in the street and in area meetings. The problem of crime seemed to transcend cultural differences and the particular interests of the separate groups. Several alternatives were proposed by the community organizers: (*a*) requesting the cooperation of the police department; (*b*) organizing direct action demanding police intervention; and (*c*) self-policing of the neighborhood. Cuban participants, most of them political refugees, who tend to be very respectful of authority, symbols of order, and the status quo, were "all the way" for requesting the cooperation of the police department. Puerto Ricans, who have experienced the effectiveness of organized pressure and advocacy within our system, voted for direct action. On the contrary, Haitians, who are fugitives of an authoritarian regime and live under a constant fear of being victims of the American immigration authorities, were more inclined to solve the problem by policing themselves. Different cultural experiences once more resulted in different ideas about problem solving, created cleavages among the several ethnic groups comprising the young Wynwood Neighborhood Organization.

Another social reality that we have confirmed in our initial efforts to organize a multiethnic association is the fact that nobody wants to lose or change cultural identity. In the very beginning we made the mistake of emphasizing too much the integrative nature of the organization. The reaction, especially among the White Americans still living in the area, was immediate and strong. They did not want to learn another language. They said they did not like integration. Some of them expressed antipathy for cultural patterns of some of the other groups sharing their physical territory.

One more time we experienced at the local level the need for cultural identity. It is a precious possession that no one wants to lose. The persistence of natural clusters is a means of securing this identity.

We might conclude that integration of programs into multiracial or multiethnic ones seems to be just a dream, a myth, or only a utopia. If we want collaboration in common actions, perhaps we must maximize the ethnic differences and orchestrate a variety of approaches to problem solving. American society is rich in cultural diversity. We live and work within a pluralistic and multiethnic society, but, as we have observed, few groups are willing to give up their cultural identity.

My solution to the problem is that organizers and agencies stop fighting natural clusters and start accepting the diversity of ethnic groups. In addition, I suggest that we utilize to the maximum the riches of cultural differences. How do we use cultural differences and natural clusters in community organization? First, we must show respect for cultural differences. We must learn to express our respect in a very explicit manner at every opportunity, in our family visits and in our street meetings. We must try not only to verbalize but also to show and to practice genuine respect. We are then saying that, yes, we are calling all of the groups to collaborate in common actions toward recovering political power and making democracy work, but we are also saying that we expect everyone to work toward this through his or her own ethnic and cultural group. People seem to feel safe in diversity when they are assured that their individuality and their culture will be respected and preserved. We are learning that only then are people of different ethnic backgrounds ready for communication and collaboration. Otherwise, they reject organizational integration.

Another factor that seems to be very important in working effectively in a multiethnic neighborhood is the maintenance of a relative numerical balance among groups in order to create mutual confidence and trust.

In community organization numbers are equal to power. When people see themelves at a numerical disadvantage in relation to other groups, they perceive themselves as powerless and become distrustful and non-cooperative. They know that they will be used now, and then later left out by the majorities. We have not been successful in obtaining this numerical balance in our neighborhood organization, for instance, with respect to the Haitian constituency. Haitian participation in our neighborhood organizational activities is low because Haitians have no culturally based organization; there are indications, however, that an effective Haitian community group can be put together. It is my experience that they cluster, they are concerned, and they will discuss neighborhood problems as long as only Haitians are present.

A related technique which may facilitate communications among different ethnic groups is the use of persons who are "natural cross-links." By this term I mean the relatively few group members who have the ability to get out of their own group clusters and go into those of other groups. Usually these link persons are vocal, and in some cases they are multilingual. As a rule they are open, charming, and very sociable individuals. These natural cross-links prove to be key leaders in attempting to overcome cultural barriers. In most cases they are highly visible; they visit and have friends who do not belong to their own ethnic group; they cross the street and talk over the fence to "other" neighbors of a different color or race; and they volunteer to be interpreters when the community organizer encounters language problems in communicating. They open doors that otherwise would be closed. The most relevant characteristic the organizer looks for among natural cross-links is the ability to produce people, to have a following. Link persons are not necessarily leaders. Leaders have several important characteristics that differentiate them from the rest. A few natural cross-links, however, are also good leaders.

The leader-links play an especially important role because they not only help to break the ice, but they also help their followers to appreciate and participate in a holistic approach to community organization. They are able to sell ideas and bring people into meetings and common activities. These leader-links are responsible not only for the breaking of natural clusters but also for crossing over and maintaining a flow of people between the different groups.

The natural cross-links who are not leaders are nevertheless valuable in making initial contacts and establishing dialogue between cultural groups, and their talents can be utilized by the community organizer to increase information flow about how the different culture-based organizations plan to attack a common problem.

Throughout this chapter I have been suggesting that organizers and agencies need not be afraid to admit cultural differences. Indeed, it is unhealthy to try to hide these differences. Rather, we must seek to make each separate group aware of cultural distinctions that may result in differences of method and action by other groups.

In the Wynwood Neighborhood Organization our attempt has been to use multiple means to achieve a common goal, rather than to expect the geographical community to agree on a plan and then automatically act as a whole. We have come to expect people to use different methods to solve problems, depending on their cultural backgrounds. In order to be successful in a multiethnic neighborhood, we must permit every group to tackle each problem in that group's own way. In other words, we must use different cultural experiences and abilities to the maximum in a coordinated effort to solve common problems. The critical task is to create mutual appreciation for the different activities undertaken by each separate cultural group toward the common goal.

The final stage of community organization is achieved when the organizer is able to phase out and the multiethnic groups are able to maintain the flow of communication and coordinated action on their own. This happens only when trust and respect exist among all the cluster groups involved, when some leader-links have been accepted by all groups, and when enough actions have taken place to serve as a binding agent among them all. One important key is communication overlap between many groups rather than amalgamation of groups into one organization. Majority constituencies, not isolated organized minorities, will bring power back to the people.

We are dealing with a pluralistic society in which ethnic groups have not only different, but also sometimes antagonistic, methods of solving problems. If we really want to build working coalitions, therefore, we must encourage awareness and appreciation of the cultural differences and methods of others. We must help groups work together on the basis of natural clusters and not try to force artificial integration by breaking these clusters down. We must train ourselves to create networks of small culture-based organizations as a workable alternative to centralized organizations with so-called representation of different ethnic groups.

Our society is pluralistic and multiethnic. On one hand, cultural identity is crucial for poor people, since it is one of the few possessions they have left. On the other hand, different ethnic values and experiences sometimes result in conflictive methods about doing things and solving problems. I am suggesting, therefore, that, instead of fighting natural clusters in attempting to integrate peoples who are different, we attempt collective and coordinated actions to solve common problems, using to the maximum the different cultural abilities and experiences of groups of people living within certain geographical boundaries.

NOTES

1. I want to express my gratitude to Mrs. Virginia H. Hine, distinguished and supersensitive scholar, writer, and professor, who assisted me in putting my experiences in an academic perspective.
2. *Co-opt* is used in the community organization jargon to refer to the process by which the system absorbs, buys up, or appropriates indigenous leadership.
3. Boundaries for Wynwood area are: south, N.W. 20th Street; north, N.W. 36th Street; east, N.E. 2nd Avenue; west, N.W. 7th Avenue.
4. Survey conducted by Puerto Rican Opportunity Center, 1977.
5. Survey conducted by Borinquen Health Care Center, 1976.

REFERENCES

Alinsky, Saul, 1963. Verbatim reprint of notes on an untitled lecture presented before the State Conference of the Washington Association for Social Welfare (Tacoma, Wash.: Washington Association for Social Welfare).
Borinquen Health Care Center, 1976. Borinquen Health Care Center—Budget Revision 1977–78 (unpublished paper prepared for submission to the Department of Health, Education and Welfare).
De Leeuw, Bert, 1974. Learning to Build Majority Organizations. *Just Economics* 2 (1) : 2.
Gerlach, Luther P., and Virginia H. Hine, 1970. *People, Power, Change: Movements of Social Transformation* (Indianapolis: Bobbs-Merrill).
Miller, Mike, 1974. *Putting People Power in Action: Reader in Mass Organization* (San Francisco, Cal.: Organize, Inc.).
Puerto Rican Opportunity Center, 1977. *Wynwood: Perspectives on a Multi-Cultural Community* (pamphlet published by the Puerto Rican Opportunity Center).
Rothstein, Richard, 1973. *Reader in Mass Organization* (Chicago: Midwest Academy).

Ethnic Communication Circuits and Noise in a Rural Community in Tanzania

Joseph V. Guillotte III

A great deal of the content of interethnic communication is political. The very nature of ethnicity, emphasizing certain roles to the exclusion of others, insures that loyalty to one's own ethnic group at least implicitly connotes competition with another group, especially when resources are scarce. This study analyzes the communication problems and solutions of a multiethnic speech community, Magugu, as well as two speech communities, the Mbugwe and Barabaig, which are opposed to it. I use Gumperz's definition of a speech community: "a social group which may be either monolingual or multilingual—held together by frequency of social interaction patterns and set off from the surrounding areas by weaknesses in the lines of communication" (Gumperz 1962 : 30).

Linguistic considerations are becoming increasingly important in political anthropology. In recent studies of ethnically heterogenous communities, or homogenous communities in the context of the nation state, it has become necessary to examine the political role of language.

The two domains of language and politics are so closely connected that in many cases they are indistinguishable. Languages are deliberately used as tools of power. Both legitimate and illegitimate means of obtaining and exercising power short of violence involve language (Knappert 1968 : 60). Language is often indicative of boundaries between groups. This boundary-forming aspect is especially important in multilingual communities of the type described in this paper.

One way of presenting sociolinguistic data from Magugu is in light of the communication theory of Claude E. Shannon. This theory developed from an attempt to solve problems in the field of electrical communication, but Edmonson and others have demonstrated that it can be used in the presentation of cultural data.

Shannon's proof appears to come closest to conceptualizing what a minimal theory of cultural structure might involve: the differentiation of structure from randomness or of news from noise. The theory diagrams the procedure of sending a signal through a channel (Edmonson 1971:

49). In brief, a communication system involves an information source, a transmitter, a channel, a receiver, and a destination (Weaver 1966 : 17). The information source selects a desired message from a set of possible messages. The transmitter changes this into a signal, which is then sent over a communication channel to the receiver. The receiver is a sort of inverse transmitter, which changes the transmitted signal back into a message and hands it on to the destination. Unfortunately, noise or unintended elements are added to the signal. These may be distortions of sound, static errors in transmission, and many other things that will be suggested below. In brief, all changes in a signal may be called noise (Weaver 1966 : 15).

As far as political communication is concerned, we should consider two other factors that are not outlined in Shannon's schema: meaning and influence. Weaver has simplified the definition of communication to "include all the procedures by which one mind can affect another" (Weaver 1966 : 15).

The concept of noise merits further discussion. The general dictionary defines noise as a sound, usually a disagreeable or abusive one. When we stress the communication theory definition—"extraneous currents . . . always present to interfere with the signals sent," or Weaver's definition above—we are led to a broader view of the subject of noise and one that has application to interethnic communication.

We might reasonably amend the definition not only to consider noise intereference with the channel but with any other part of the communication system. Time may be noise to the historian or archeologist. Status differences may be noise to the citizen trying to speak to a higher-status political figure. Distance can also be noise. Noise is a universal factor in human communication. It might be considered a constant. There is no reason to suspect that noise should be absent or diminished in a linguistic situation. The variation in individual experiences within a cultural communication system would in itself be a form of noise. Smith has suggested that redundancy, which overcomes noise, is impossible in this context since "each successive reception of the same signal changes the decoding of that signal. To some extent, the same signal cannot be received more than once" (Smith 1966 : 9).

Not only is experiential variation one of the noise problems in human communication, but also language difference is a problem, as we see often in the interethnic or multiethnic communication situation. In this situation, a receiver that in normal communication is "a sort of inverse transmitter" having the capacity to accommodate a specific frequency is replaced by a receiver that does not have this capacity. Human receiver and transmitter can accommodate themselves to this situation by (*a*) changing to a mutually accommodative frequency; (*b*) substituting components, that is, learning a third language (for example, Swahili, as demonstrated in the following cases); or (*c*) learning each other's language. Until one of these is done, an extremely noisy situation prevails. Certainly some information can still be communicated before this is done, but myth or lore cannot.

If communication and culture are inseparable, then so are noise and culture. In fact, one might say that all culture is an attempt to circumvent noise. The attempt is never wholly successful. "Noise in culture" might be seen as simply another way of expressing the concept of culture change. Noise is the source of creativity and the death of custom. It is a filter that strains the acceptable signals and forces changes in the capacities of receiver and transmitter. A perfect communication system without noise would be a monotonous communication circuit. A signal once generated would reverberate endlessly.

LINGUISTIC COMMUNICATION IN MAGUGU

Magugu is a rural community in the Arusha region of northern Tanzania. It is a branch territory of the Tanganyika African National Union (TANU), the solitary legitimate political party in Tanzania. In its population of about seven thousand are represented over eighty tribal groups within an eight-hundred-mile radius. The residents are for the most part dispersed over one hundred and fifty square miles, with the exception of one thousand who live in Kibaoni, a small town that straddles the Great North Road ninety miles south of Arusha.

In 1944, a sleeping sickness outbreak occurred among the labor force on European estates a few miles south of the present location of Kibaoni. The colonial administration ordered the immediate evacuation and quarantine of these African workers. After the quarantine period the evacuees were offered the choice of either being transported to their tribal homelands or settling down, clearing bush, and forming a new community at Magugu to hinder the northward spread of the tsetse fly, the vector of the disease. About one thousand chose to remain and become the nucleus of the polyethnic community.

The settlement was located on land that was nominally the territory of the Mbugwe tribe, and the new community was placed under the authority of the Mbugwe paramount chief. The migrants elected a headman, and a native authority and treasury were formed. For all practical purposes, however, Magugu was a separate polity largely ignored by both the colonial administration and the Mbugwe hierarchy. Local government was, for the most part, independent of the Mbugwe power structure except for the referral of major criminal cases which were heard by the Mbugwe judiciary. This relative political independence continued for the first ten years of the settlement's existence.

From the founding of the settlement until the time of my field study (1969–1970), there had existed mutual antipathy and animosity between the largely Moslem settler population and the Mbugwe. This hard feeling was exacerbated in 1954 when the Mbugwe made an effort to take over the heretofore semi-independent political structure of the Magugu. At this time, the last paramount chief of the Mbugwe succeeded in having his brother appointed the headman of Magugu. He had the former Moslem headman who was elected by the emigrant population arrested for theft. In 1956 the first TANU organizers came to Magugu, and the newly formed independence party spread rapidly among the migrant population in spite of resistance from the Mbugwe chief and the colonial authorities. After independence in 1961, the role of chief was abolished in Tanzania. Magugu then replaced the Mbugwe neighborhood as the center of governmental activity, services, and patronage in the area. Kibaoni became the division headquarters as well as the site of the division magistracy and the location for a twenty-eight-bed hospital.

Magugu and the area within a hundred miles of it are peopled by speakers of all the language families of Africa; however, the majority of the tongues of Tanzania and this region fall into the Bantu subdivision of the Benue-Congo subfamily of the Niger-Kordofanian family (Greenberg 1966: 8, 9, 49, 72, 85, 177). This includes Swahili, the coastal Arabic-Bantu Creole that has become the national language of Tanzania and is so important to Magugu. *Kiswahili*, the Swahili language, has a long and complex history that has been recently well-researched by Whitely (1969). *Waswahili*, the Swahili people, is a term with a more complex derivation and application. In the Magugu area *Waswahili* are, in the eyes of the Mbugwe, those people who inhabit Magugu and especially Kibaoni. Very few of these people were actually born on the coast, but most are Moslems and all are *wageni* or strangers to the Mbugwe. The term is a political one to the Mbugwe. It labels an ethnically heterogenous population whose leaders have been traditionally opposed to Mbugwe interests. The people of Magugu refer to the Mbugwe as *washenzi* ("boorish barbarians"); by their tribal name; as *wapagani* ("pagans"); or by other less amicable terms. They refer to themselves as *waswahili* or by their specific tribal names.

SWAHILI AS AN INTEGRATIVE MECHANISM

The conclusions presented here derive from a language survey made during the course of the 1969–1970 field study. The groups surveyed were approximately half of the population of Kibaoni and the majority of the population of Bondeni, a settlement a few miles to the north of Kibaoni. Bondeni is outside the boundary of Magugu's TANU branch but part of the Mbugwe division. Settlement began in the late 1940's after the founding of Kibaoni. It is predominantly an Mbugwe neighborhood, but twenty-four other tribal groups are represented in its population. Kibaoni is the more heterogenous area, with at least forty-six African languages spoken there. The total number of individuals in the Kibaoni sample is 597; there were 505 in the Bondeni sample.

In the whole survey of 1,108 people, only 2 claimed not to speak any Swahili. In Kibaoni, 25 percent of the children speak only Swahili (83 of 330). In Bondeni, 4½ percent of the children speak Swahili exclusively (13 of 295). This 25 percent monolingualism in Swahili in Kibaoni should be looked upon as a conservative estimate rather than an accurate figure. The survey data were collected from adults, usually the parents of the children. These parents, I observed, were often carried away with enthusiasm when describing their children's linguistic competence. One woman, an Irangi married to a Sambaa, for example, told me that her children could speak the three languages in the household—Irangi, Sambaa, and Swahili. When I questioned these children away from their mother's presence, they positively stated that they could only speak Swahili, although they did know a few greetings in the other languages. Of twenty Kibaoni children between the ages of five and ten whom I questioned, only one claimed to speak another tongue besides Swahili and that only superficially.

There is a strong contrast in the mobility of the populations of Bondeni and Kibaoni. Only 12 percent of the Kibaoni adults were born there (30 of 287). This is in dramatic contrast with Bondeni, where 62 percent of the adults were indigenous to the community (131 of 210). This contrast substantiates in part impressions gained from the examination of other data, that is, that geographical mobility—the experience of moving across tribal and regional boundaries—is more congruent with receptivity to national ideas than is nonmobility—or remaining in the country of one's birth. At the very least, the physical horizons of the individual are widened and he or she is taken out of a group that might compete with national interests. Such mobility also implies more recourse to the national language. To maneuver out of one's tribal area, one must often communicate with other groups through the use of Swahili. The Kibaoni settlers' travel experience contrasts with that of the Mbugwe, who have a reputation for insularity. Out of a sample of twenty Mbugwe males, ten had never left their tribal area, five had left for short periods of time—in all cases less than a year—and five had stayed for over a year.

In Kibaoni there is a tendency for the adult settlers to retain the language of their tribal homelands and use Swahili for everyday communication. However, in Bondeni there is also linguistic incorporation into the local group, the Mbugwe. The number who speak Kimbugwe in addition to the national tongue and their own tribal languages indicates that because of the more homogenous ethnic makeup in Bondeni, there is a tendency to use the local language. Such localism can give rise to one problem where nationalism is concerned: it ties the speaker to a network that in many cases is antithetical or at least trivial to the nationalist. In Kibaoni, less than 14 percent speak Kimbugwe. In Bondeni, 55 percent (or 365 people) speak the local vernacular. Of these Kimbugwe speakers, only 107 are adults who claim affiliation with the Mbugwe tribe. The 258 remaining speakers are either: (*a*) adults from other tribal groups who have learned Kimbugwe since they moved to Bondeni (10); or (*b*) children of Mbugwe and spouses of other ethnic groups (217); or (*c*) people who claim affiliation with other tribal groups but who were born in Bondeni (31).

There is a similar incorporative process occurring in both communities. In Kibaoni, children tend to learn the national language to the exclusion of tribal vernaculars. Indeed, the local language of Kibaoni and the national language are the same. Local and national communication circuits are congruent. In Bondeni non-Mbugwe children tend to learn the local vernacular in addition to the national language. In Kibaoni, vernaculars are lost rather than learned, but in Bondeni, Kimbugwe is adopted by immigrants and is also the vernacular of children whether or not their parents are Mbugwe.

The people of Kibaoni are very much aware of the role of Swahili in giving their community a degree of cohesion in spite of a multiethnic population. In the terms of communication theory, it might be said that they see Swahili as a circuit that is necessary for overcoming the "noisy" multilingual, multicomplex circuits. They also see Swahili as being related to a different political process than the former parochial Mbugwe hegemony, a connection with citizenship rather than tribalism. A general conclusion is that the people of Kibaoni have closer ties to the national government than do the people of Bondeni. A significant number of young people have not acquired any other language than the national language. Their interests are attached to pantribal or nontribal linguistic symbols since they cannot communicate with any other linguistic communities except through the medium of the national language. They are forced to be part of the national communication circuit. This monolingualism in the national tongue denies them participation in activities that require a knowledge of another tongue; among these activities is tribal politics. The national orientation also applies to Magugu adults. Although they still retain their tribal tongues, while they reside in Magugu they must use the national language.

The incidence of Swahili varies between the two communities. In Kibaoni, the only way the individuals from the two different language groups can communicate is through the use of the national tongue. However, in Bondeni and in other Mbugwe neighborhoods, Kimbugwe is spoken whenever possible. Even Mbugwe drinking together in a Kibaoni beer hall will use their own language rather than Swahili. At times deliberately, at times unconsciously, they retreat behind an ethnolinguistic wall.

O'Barr, studying Asu-speaking Pare, stated that the Pare consider their language as a residual language "continuing to be used where Swahili has yet to make an incursion." The Pare say "that Swahili is an introduced language and serves in introduced situations, and that Asu is the indigenous language and serves in traditional situations" (O'Barr 1971 : 298). This is comparable to Mbugwe attitudes toward their own language. Swahili is associated with nation, rather than tribe, with government and social service, schools and literacy, foreigners and commerce, a general enlargement of social and valuational scale rather than parochial interests. Swahili has the weight of government approval and encouragement and is the dominant language in the neighborhood. However, this study indicates that in certain situations like that which occurs in Bondeni, where a few outsiders have settled in an ethnically homogenous area, the local vernacular remains important in interethnic communication.

In Anderson's terms, cultural integration is a process of the reduction of variants, or alternative elements (Anderson 1960 : 52). Magugu presents us with a formidable array of variants in behavior and language. The widespread usage of Swahili reduces communicative variants by providing a communication circuit for all members of the community. The national language displaces tribal tongues for all public occasions and for most private interaction, especially in the intertribal marital situation.

Of a sample of conjugal households 39 percent in the Magugu area indicated spouses who were of different ethnic origins (290 of 748). The very existence of this phenomenon is, of course, another indicator of social and cultural integration underway in the community. Such a demonstrable policy of outmarriage, as Goody has observed for Gonja, leads to a mutual adjustment of domestic relations and results in a kinship organization based upon the lowest common denominator. The result is a kind of "bilateral" system of ordering relationships for which Swahili kinship terminology provides appropriate terms (Goody 1970 : 126; Arens 1970: 184–186).

This intertribal marriage is almost synonymous with Islam; 75 percent of these marriages are between Moslems. Islam is thus another axis of social and cultural integration in the community, a world religious environment that encourages the formation of a supratribal community based on the common denominator of religion and the Swahili language. This religious homogenization occurred in the very beginning of the community and is an example of the reduction of religious variants.

Overlying the whole social structure of Magugu is the TANU political organization, based on the ten-household cell unit. Every person in the community is part of a governmental interactive web. Yet, fluency in Swahili is the essential preadaptation for all these other axes of social and cultural integration. Swahili in Magugu is thus seen as being critically important in the social, religious, political, and economic life of the population.

Einar Haugen has discussed the formation of a national language in the light of four processes: (*a*) selection of the norm; (*b*) codification of the norm (or minimal variation in form); (*c*) elaboration of maximal variation in function; and (*d*) acceptance by the populace (Haugen 1966: 929–933). In Tanzania, the first two processes took place at the colonial and national governmental level with the choice of Swahili as a lingua franca by the Germans, British, and independent governments of Tanzania and the work of the International Swahili Committee in its codification of the dialect of Zanzibar. Although policy decisions concerning language planning can be made in the centers of power, before a language can be a viable national tongue, the last two processes must also be accomplished at the village level.

The elaboration of function or application of the language to a variety of social and cultural exigencies is critical, since a national language must be the common language of a group more complex and inclusive than those using vernaculars. It must answer to the needs of many communities, classes, occupations, and interest groups. In Magugu, Swahili has become the language for every aspect of the life of what I would term a "national community" to distinguish it from a tribal community such as the Mbugwe, who prefer to use their own vernacular whenever possible.

Finally, Swahili is accepted by the community. This acceptance is more statistically important in Kibaoni where definite tendencies toward monolingualism are noted; however, even the more parochially oriented Mbugwe demonstrate acceptance of Swahili as a second language out of necessity (Haugen 1966; Whiteley 1969 : 3–4, 59, 61).

It would seem that Magugu is a microcosm of the national Tanzanian poltico-linguistic system. Language groups proliferate throughout Tanzania as in Magugu. However, the national system is made up of many dual systems such as the Mbugwe possess. Speakers of vernaculars speak their language and resort to the national language only when they are forced to do so in educational, political, and other introduced situations. The national system consists of messages in Swahili that come down from Dar es Salaam to regional, area, divisional, and branch levels of the Tanzanian government and of messages emanating from these levels that are sent to the national capital. In the process of sending and receiving these messages, the government encounters many language barriers: noise. To overcome these barriers, two alternatives can be chosen: (*a*) messages can be translated into the local language; (*b*) both sender and receiver can use the national language. Alternative (*a*) is for the most part unacceptable as well as impractical, although in some cases it is necessary, as the following situation among the Barabaig exemplifies.

THE MANIPULATION OF LANGUAGE IN INTERETHNIC CONFRONTATION

I have thus far emphasized the necessity of using Swahili by all people in Magugu and by the Mbugwe some of the time. All these people are sedentary horticulturists and livestock keepers. There is another segment of the population that has emerged in the past few years. This is the Barabaig, a group of pastoralists who have left their traditional homeland about fifty miles to the southwest to "follow the grass" to the environs of Magugu and Mbugwe. They began to move into the Magugu neighborhood in 1967. For the most part, they shun contact with the farmers of the area and graze their stock on the outskirts of the community.

In the early part of 1970, the people and government officials of Magugu were incensed over reports that the Barabaig were stealing livestock and produce and destroying garden plots. The Barabaig were also allegedly using strong-arm methods to force people to buy their milk.

The TANU chairman and assistant divisional executive officer of Magugu called a public meeting to which were summoned several of the Barabaig elders. The meeting was held outdoors under a baobab tree in the neighborhood where most of the alleged outrages had occurred. It was attended by several hundred of the Magugu settlers, including many Mbugwe who were openly siding with the settlers in this situation. The Barabaig were represented by five elders and a youth.

Although all of the accusations and discussions were made in Swahili, the Barabaig elders claimed not to speak the language, and the youth acted as interpreter. When the elders proclaimed the innocence of their people, they did so in their own language. They were able to withdraw into another symbol system and in a sense to avoid direct confrontation. The government communication system had broken down here. The national information source had to use the channel and transmitter of another system. Noise came not from interference with a channel, but from the receiver and transmitter. The audience was infuriated with the strategy of the Barabaig.

Usually these types of meetings are extremely formal. Individuals who have something to say—even though in everyday life that person might be the village idiot or the man who swabs out the local saloon—are accorded respect. One rises, shouts a political slogan—to which the refrain is invariably droned by the audience, *Kazi ya TANU* ("the work of TANU")—and then portentously proclaims his or her question or observation. The chairman of the meeting seriously considers the offering and then gives his own opinion or answer. The normal protocol was suspended, however, whenever a Barabaig spoke or was translated for. Barabaig protestations of innocence were received with hoots and cries of derision. It was as if the people knew that noise was being inserted deliberately into the governmental system. Indeed, I know that it was.

At a later date, I spoke to some of the elders who had previously denied a knowledge of Swahili. Their Swahili at this time was certainly adequate. As all had suspected at the meeting, the elders had elected at a crucial moment of confrontation between tribe and nation to identify with tribe by pleading ignorance of the national tongue. As far as the government was concerned, the result was the same as if the Barabaig had not spoken Swahili. A translator was used and there was a certain distance held between the accused and accusers. It was an example of the manipulation of language in a political situation. At this time, Barabaig "language policy" constituted rejection of the national language.

Another example of the Barabaig manipulation of the national language was reported to me a few years later and reveals a contrasting posture. Since the first incursion of the Barabaig into the Magugu area, they had proceeded to drift farther to the north and into Mbugwe territory. There, again, their reputations made them the alleged perpetrators of every case of thievery and assault that took place in the neighborhood. In January of 1972, Mbugwe elders decided that they were fed up with the presence of the Barabaig and they decided to ask them to leave. They called a meeting with the Barabaig elders and told them that they should leave the Mbugwe country. If the Barabaig refused, the Mbugwe would appeal to the government, and the Mbugwe assured the strangers that they would be transported away by force. Again, the Barabaig claimed to be innocent of any wrongdoing. They insisted that they were being blamed for crimes that others had committed. Furthermore, they stated that the Mbugwe did not have any authority to even ask them to leave the country since Barabaig as well as Mbugwe were all citizens of Tanzania and as citizens had the right to reside wherever they pleased. Eventually the local government officials heard of this case and essentially reiterated the Barabaig's stand on freedom of movement of all citizens (Mbee 1972).

In this latter situation, the Barabaig opted to claim national rights as citizens of Tanzania. The Mbugwe had also reversed their policy. In the first case, they were siding with local government officials and, implicitly, with national interests. In the second case, they wanted to approach the Barabaig on a tribal basis, essentially asserting traditional tribal territoriality. In the second case, both Barabaig and Mbugwe spoke Swahili. I believe the use of Swahili by the Barabaig was more than an expedient use of a lingua franca for interethnic communication. Associating themselves with a national language was a deliberate ploy in buttressing their claim to citizenship and freedom of movement throughout the country. If the Barabaig had chosen to speak their own tongue in this situation, I do not believe that there would have been any problem of language communication. There are many Barabaig-speaking Mbugwe who could have performed as interpreters. There are Mbugwe who have Barabaig forebears who migrated to Mbugwe and were incorporated into the tribe within recent memory. Until the incidents cited occurred, the Mbugwe looked upon the Barabaig as friends. This was especially true where there were large concentrations of Mbugwe of Barabaig descent.

I have mentioned that there are two alternatives open to the government when encountering the noise of different languages. The first alternative is translation of messages into the local vernacular. The government's second alternative when it encounters a language barrier is to encourage both parties to use the national language. This is the usual course followed in governmental communication. All political meetings held in the Magugu area are conducted in Swahili. This is true whether the participants are the multiethnic Magugu settlers or the Mbugwe. There is a difference in the attitudes toward the national language usage, however. The Magugu settlers realize that Swahili is a practical necessity, as is any lingua franca in a multilingual situation. The Mbugwe resent having to speak Swahili when only Mbugwe speakers are gathered for a political meeting. They seem to perceive, more than do the Magugu settlers, that this government policy is a tacit statement that loyalties to a tribal language are antithetical to national loyalties because they represent loyalties to a potentially rival political system.

In Magugu, the density of the multilingual population reinforces the emphasis on the national language. National myths such as *ujamaa*, or Tanzanian socialism, and national organizations must be considered more than in other ethnically and linguistically homogenous areas because there are no conflicting symbol systems that are supportive of a competitive political structure. This does not mean that the people of Magugu are ardent patriots. Generally, they are rather apathetic toward national and local politics and merely respond to government suggestions and orders without initiating much political action themselves. Nevertheless, they do not encounter distractions—other well-organized mythic and communication systems—such as is the case with the Mbugwe and Barabaig.

SUMMARY

I have described several "language policies." First, the Tanzanian national language policy emphasizes the priority of Swahili over other languages. Because of the multiethnic Babel of Magugu, this national policy is accepted and implemented at the village level. Second, I have discussed the "language policies" of two tribal groups, the Mbugwe and the Barabaig. Although their own vernaculars are badges of ethnic identification and usually take priority over the national language, the tribespeople by no means inflexibly adhere to this priority but adjust to the needs of interethnic communication situations.

We can determine that there are two processes being carried out concurrently. First, there is the phenomenon of homogenization or the subsuming of diversity under such common denominators as religion, political organization, and linguistic conformity. In a sense, this is a creolization process, the domestic assembly and combining of foreign components. At the same time, there continues another significant process as the Mbugwe and Barabaig maintain their distinctiveness. The speech community of the Mbugwe is being increased by immigrants who learn the vernacular and conceivably help to maintain its exclusivity. Blending of diverse elements takes place in two different types of community— the national community and the tribal community. At the time of my research, there did not seem to be any indication that one type would eclipse the other.

REFERENCES

Anderson, Robert, 1960. Reduction of Variants as a Measure of Cultural Integration. In *Essays in the Science of Culture*, Gertrude Dole and Robert Carneiro, eds. (New York: Thomas Y. Crowell), pp. 50–62.
Arens, William E., 1970. *Mto Wa Mbu: A Study of a Multitribal Community in Rural Tanzania* (Ph.D. dissertation, University of Virginia).
Edmonson, Munro S., 1971. *Lore: An Introduction to the Science of Folklore and Literature* (New York: Holt, Rinehart, and Winston).
Goody, Jack, 1970. Marriage Policy and Incorporation in Northern Ghana. In *From Tribe to Nation in Africa: Studies in Incorporation Processes*, Ronald Cohen and John Middleton, eds. (Scranton: Chandler Publishing), pp. 114–149.
Greenberg, Joseph H., 1966. *The Languages of Africa* (The Hague: Mouton).
Gumperz, John J., 1962. Types of Linguistic Communities. *Anthropological Linguistics* 4 : 28–40.
Haugen, Einar, 1966. Dialect, Language, Nation. *American Anthropologist* 68 : 922–935.
Knappert, Jan, 1968. The Function of Language in a Political Situation. *Linguistics* 39 : 59–67.
Mbee, Gicha, 1972. Letter to J. V. Guillotte from Magugu.
O'Barr, William M., 1971. Multilingualism in a Rural Tanzanian Village. *Anthropological Linguistics* 13 : 289–300.
Smith, Alfred G., 1966. Introduction: Communication and Culture. In *Communication and Culture: Readings in the Codes of Human Interaction*, Alfred G. Smith, ed. (New York: Holt, Rinehart, and Winston), pp. 1–10.
Weaver, Warren, 1966. The Mathematics of Communication. In *Communication and Culture: Readings in the Codes of Human Interaction*, Alfred G. Smith, ed. (New York: Holt, Rinehart, and Winston), pp. 15–24.
Whiteley, W. H., 1969. *Swahili: The Rise of a National Language* (London: Methuen).

Missionaries Among the Eastern Cherokees: Religion as a Means of Interethnic Communication

LAURENCE FRENCH

An important question in the field of ethnic studies concerns the role of religion in the process of interethnic communication. In this chapter I will examine the role of religion in majority-minority relations, specifically using the example of Indian-White interaction in the United States. Attention is focused on the Eastern Band of Cherokee Indians of western North Carolina, who have a rich, well-documented cultural heritage and who hold the unique status of being the most visited Native American group in the United States today, with an onslaught of some eight million tourists during each season of April to October. Moreover, the early nineteenth-century battle for converts on the mission field was fought between the major fundamentalist churches, the Baptist and Methodist, in the mountains of southern Appalachia, the home of the Eastern Cherokees. A changing economy has led more recently to new missionaries among the Cherokees and new competition for the now well-established Baptist church. This study examines the historical development of crucial events in the post-contact religious history of Eastern Cherokees and suggests the underlying reasons for these.

RELIGION AND SOCIAL CONTROL: A THEORETICAL PERSPECTIVE

In this study I have viewed Indian reservations as constituting "total institutions," where federal paternalism and accommodation are important factors in interethnic relations. On a continuum of types of interethnic interaction between majority and minority populations, with assimilation at one extreme and forced accommodation at the other, it could be argued that Indian reservations in the United States and reserves in Canada fall closer to the latter than to the former.

The argument that Indian reservations are in a position of total accommodation is essentially that the combination of racial visibility and and a phenomenological (folk culture) ideology leads to conditions least favorable to assimilation by the larger dominant, technological society. Interethnic communication is often strained in this type of environment. In this case the strain is due mainly to the regulatory structure used by the federal control agencies mandated to operate these reservations. The dominant control agencies subscribe to the Protestant Ethic and attempt to implement their policies through secondary, impersonal institutions, establishing and maintaining formal and rigid social and physical distance between themselves and the Indian wards they regulate. This process not only creates a one-directional communication, it generates an insurmountable communication gap between the two groups as well. This is unfortunate, since the regulatory agencies as a result seldom receive, nor solicit, needed information and feedback from those whom they are entrusted with regulating.

According to this model, the reservation system shares many of the shortcomings Goffman (1961) describes for other total institutions. Basically what happens is that a small elite of regulators determine policy in accordance with their cultural beliefs, while at the same time maintaining rigid social and physical distance between themselves and those they regulate. The irony is that these systems are nourished on their own failure. Prisons, mental institutions, and Indian reservations all have as their clients social members who are considered deficient in some respect according to the dominant normative value system. Ideally, Indian reservations are designed to prepare Native Americans to adapt to the demands of the larger dominant culture, while actually the opposite occurs. Instead of teaching independence—the primary value of the Protestant Ethic—Indian reservations foster dependency, resulting in a self-fulfilling prophecy: the more the Native Americans are subjected to the regulatory agencies, the more they become dependent upon them.

Crucial to the continuation of all these dependent institutions is the process in which the individual, upon entry, is psychologically stripped of his or her homeworld identity. Goffman (1961) describes this process for mental hospitals and prisons. For American Indians this involves the stripping away by authorities of the local traditional cultural heritage. The cultural mortification of Native Americans is a shocking history of policies ranging from physical brutality to the modern, more subtle behavioral modification programs, all with the same objective—to stress the superiority of the dominant cultural value system, American Protestant, to that of the native culture.

Initially this paradoxical situation seems to defy reason. Why is the dominant value system stressed and the native folk heritage discouraged when assimilation is not the expressed objective of the accommodative reservation system? Joseph Gusfield's (1963) analysis of the temperance movement sheds some light on this matter. In his work *Symbolic Crusade*, Gusfield alleges that public policy that seems on the surface to stress universal application may in fact be a subtle attempt to legitimize a particular belief system at the expense of others. Consequently, the attempt to legislate morality may well represent the effort of a particular group to use the law to legitimize their social elitism as well as clearly distinguish themselves from those social members they consider to be undesirable. Gusfield saw prohibition as an attempt by native White Anglo-Saxon Protestants (WASPs) legally to establish their cultural value system as being superior to that of the new immigrants, who were predominantly Catholics and Jews. Alcohol came symbolically to represent the inferiority of those religious ideologies that sanctioned this substance, i.e., Catholics and Jews. Parallels can be seen between Gusfield's example and the example of the reservation system. Both the denial of the Indian's traditional cultural heritage and the denial of acceptance to Indians in the larger dominant society leave little question as to the symbolic meaning of the Indian's inferiority and second-class status.

The relegation to a total institution makes the reservation Indian more manageable, a process Goffman illustrated in other total institutions. A dependent marginal inmate population is clearly identified, then rigid social distance is maintained between the staff (Bureau of Indian Affairs) and those regulated (reservation Indians), forbidding primary interaction between the two groups. This situation forces the inmates (those regulated) to rely on each other for primary needs. In prisons and mental institutions these are indeed artificial subcultures, while on Indian reservations some aspects of the traditional culture may still be intact. Nonetheless, continual attempts to establish legally the traditional home-world culture as being negative and unacceptable is yet another device used to perpetuate the marginal status of the reservation Indians, thus making them easier to manage.

The process of generating and maintaining a subculture of marginal Indians, forcing them between two inaccessible worlds, provides the control agents with an effective lever of control according to the Goffman model. Interestingly, missionary churches usually play an important role in maintaining these precarious majority-minority relations. This is evident not only from examples in Indian-White relations but also from examples that occurred during slavery and Reconstruction and continues today in some Black-White relations. In addition, there are examples of this in our nation's prisons and reformatories and in other places where it is necessary to stress the ideological superiority of the dominant culture vis-à-vis that of conditional minority subcultures. A look at Cherokee-White relations with an emphasis on the interaction with Protestant missionaries offers an interesting assessment of this situation, providing a traceable record from initial contact to the present.

EARLY MISSIONARIES AMONG THE CHEROKEES

Sporadic Cherokee-White relations occurred from as early as the 1540's, when DeSoto ventured into the North Carolina highlands. Permanent relations, however, were not established until the early 1700's. This White-Indian interaction also provided another type of confrontation, that between the Cherokees and other Indian groups displaced from their traditional coastal and piedmont homes by the influx of White settlers. Other Indians sought protection in Cherokee territory to avoid being caught up in the flourishing colonial Indian slave trade. It was during this same period that Whites, notably Scotch-Irish and English religious and social dissidents, started to live among the Cherokees. Evidently, mixblood population (White-Indian) emerged during the next century. This era saw a notable change in the Cherokee lifestyle, including changes in their religious belief system.

The aboriginal belief system was animistic, with nature playing a significant role. The Cherokee myth regarding their origin portrays the earth as a great island floating in a sea of water suspended from the sky by four cords linking it with the "Sky Vault," a heavenly securing device consisting of solid rock. They believed that the earth's topology was created by the Great Buzzard who roughed out mountains and valleys while the earth was still soft and wet (Mooney 1972). This was their worldview and they saw themselves as constituting the "principal people" within this world.

A corresponding "Harmony Ethic" (Thomas 1958) dictated the desirable aboriginal behavior. Avoidance and mutual obligations are the main components of this folk ethic which, incidentally, has survived to the present. Cherokees avoid giving offense in their everyday face-to-face interaction. People avoid publicly embarrassing others while at the same time they feel compelled to fulfill the wishes of friends and relatives. Hence, obligatory hospitality, public impassivity, the refusal or unwillingness to contradict, a reluctance to assume authority, and a strong sense of individual autonomy regarding personal behavior best provides a general profile of the Cherokee socialized within the Harmony Ethic.

Clearly this behavioral pattern complemented the aboriginal *gardugi* lifestyle. The *gardugi* was the cooperative agricultural system developed by the Cherokees and utilized hundreds of years prior to white contact. The estimated 20,000 aboriginal Cherokees lived in some sixty permanent cooperative farm villages of between 300 and 600 population. The matrilineal and matrilocal clan system provided the controls necessary to regulate this group of people. Thus clan regulations, established agricultural rituals, stickball competition, hunting and war parties held the Cherokees together as a people (Reid 1970).

Contact and competition with whites and other Indian groups served to disrupt this lifestyle, forcing the bulk of the Cherokees to seek an alternate society that would prove compatible with these new circumstances. From the development of tribal leadership in 1792 to forced removal in 1838, the Cherokees underwent a rapid transformation, changing from a consensual, folk society into a representative republic, one patterned after that of their new neighbor—the United States. Even the Cherokees' national constitution,, adopted in 1827, referred to the Christian God as the ultimate power in nature, as is evident in the preamble: "We, the representatives of the people of the Cherokee Nation in convention assembled, in order to establish justice, ensure tranquility, promote our common welfare, and secure to ourselves and our prosperity the blessing of liberty; acknowledging with humility and gratitude the goodness of his sovereign Ruler of the Universe, in offering as an opportunity so favorable to the design, and imploring His aid and direction in its accomplishment, do ordain and establish this Constitution for the Government of the Cherokee Nation" (Malone 1956 : 85).

The Christian influence among the Cherokees coincided, for the most part, with the emergence of fundamentalism in America. While a rash of new fundamentalist sects sprouted in this country during the early 1800's—including the Mormons, the Pentecostals, Shakers, and the Oneida Communty—to mention a few, two fundamentalist sects greatly influenced the Cherokees: the Baptists and Methodists. Although fundamentalism has a long history, it was the frontier adaptation of this movement in the United States by the Methodists and the similar fundamental doctrines of the Baptists that led to the unique religious experience now universally recognized in the Southern Bible Belt (Snook 1973). This religious movement especially affected the Appalachian Cherokees, since it was here that the early fundamentalist missionaries sought their converts—first among the early White religious dissidents (Scotch-Irish, English, and Germans), then among the Cherokees, and later, after the Civil War, among the Black freedmen.

First the Reverend Humphrey Posey established the Locust Old Field

Baptist church in the late 1700's in southwestern North Carolina. This soon became known as the "Mother Church," from which missionaries would carry the word of salvation to Whites and Indians isolated in the Appalachian mountains, which was at this time still Cherokee territory. The Methodists soon followed, and in 1810 the Reverend Asbury, the first United States bishop of Methodism, initiated "camp meetings" in Haywood County, which bordered along the eastern frontier of the Cherokee Nation in what is now North Carolina (Bruce 1974). Both churches held similar goals for the Appalachian people—an emotional commitment to new converts and a revitalization of those already committed to Christ. In the camp meetings, singings and personal testimonies were employed for the purpose of converting lost souls to Christianity, that is, for the people to "receive the Holy Spirit" and "accept Christ as their personal saviour." The festival atmosphere helped attract these people to the camp meetings, where tents and wagons created an instant village of those gathered to give praise to the Lord. Emotions ran high and a common sound was that of the singing of "Amazing Grace," a song written by the English clergyman John Newton, a contemporary of John Wesley. This emotional environment and this song are still an integral aspect of contemporary Appalachian fundamentalism.

The Methodist and Baptist churches differed over a few issues—notably baptism and the qualifications of the clergy. The Baptists insisted on total immersion, while the Methodists did not. Moreover, the Methodists insisted upon ordained clergy, while the Baptists relied upon "the calling" for their preachers. These differences led to an historic moral battle in the 1830's in southern Appalachia, right in the heart of Cherokee territory. The Baptists, represented by the Reverend Mr. Posey, finally won a decisive moral victory over the Methodists, led by Parson Brownlow. Eventually the Baptists, who had only eight churches at the time, greatly outnumbered the Methodists, who had eleven churches in southern Appalachia.

As the Cherokee Nation developed, the Baptists and Methodists were soon joined by the Moravians and Quakers. The eventual removal of over 16,000 Cherokees (95 percent of the population) west of the Mississippi River into what was then known as Indian Territory (now Oklahoma) ended this era of early missionary work among these Indians. The fundamentalist Baptist church survived among the White settlers of southern Appalachia, while new religious associations were maintained among the Civilized Tribes (Cherokee, Choctaw, Creek, Chickasaw, and Seminole) once relocated in Indian Territory (Collier 1973).

The New Echota Treaty of 1835 spared those Appalachian Cherokees who wished to remain east, providing they deeded their land and petitioned for North Carolina citizenship. About one-third of the Appalachian Cherokees (1,000) remained behind. These were mostly traditional fullblood Cherokees, those who were most adamantly opposed to the changing of the old ways. Overall, the Appalachian Cherokees had the fewest non-Indians (Whites or Blacks) living among them at the time of removal. They also were opposed to the development of the Cherokee Nation (Bauer 1970). The mountains of North Carolina soon became the central location for those Indians spared removal. In 1840 one hundred Catawba Indians joined the Eastern Cherokees, while a number of mixblood Cherokees apparently filtered back into southern Appalachia from Indian Territory. The proportion of mixbloods increased within the thirteen years following removal. By the time of the Civil War some 1,700 Eastern Cherokees resided in the North Carolina mountains. It was after the Civil War that federal intervention occurred, and in 1868 the Eastern Cherokees officially became wards of the federal government. This same year the tribe adopted the Lloyd Welch Constitution. Then in 1889 they were granted "corporate" status by the North Carolina legislature, and in 1924 the 56,500-acre Eastern Band came under federal trust, making it an Indian reservation.

When Thomas Donaldson, expert special agent for the United States Census Office, visited the Eastern Band in 1892 he noted that while most of the educational endeavors developed under the Cherokee Nation were now virtually nonexistent, the Christian religion seemed to have survived among these isolated Indians: "The superstitions and religious extravaganzas of ancient times have almost disappeared. Lingering fancies as to witches and witchcraft crop out from time to time among these Indians, but in no more reasonable forms than among their (white) neighbors. . . . While the people as a whole are Christian in theory and no pagan element remains, the early mission enterprises among the Cherokees have not advanced with the intelligence and physical prosperity of the people. Both Baptists and Methodists early occupied the field and with marked success. . . . There are no Catholics among the Cherokees" (Donaldson 1892).

Things remained stable until the mid-1940's when the Cherokee economy underwent a drastic transformation, from agricultural subsistence to a tourist economy. This opened the once-isolated Cherokees to new influences, exposing them to a wide variety of people other than those to whom they were accustomed (for example, in the past, government officials and mountain Whites, who were as isolated and provincial as the Cherokees themselves). Consequently, this change also brought new missionaries seeking converts among the Cherokees.

THE CONTEMPORARY MISSIONARIES
AMONG THE EASTERN CHEROKEES

The changed economy was accompanied by psychocultural changes, best illustrated by the increased number of "marginal Cherokees," those who no longer identify with their traditional folk culture. The old cooperative system coupled with physical and social isolation resulted in the preservation of the traditional aboriginal ways by the Eastern Cherokees. Most Cherokees residing in either Snow Bird Community (Graham County) or on the Qualla Boundary Community (Swain and Jackson counties) were traditional Cherokees, with a considerable degree (half or more) of Indian blood. Southern Appalachian fundamentalism facilitated their traditional lifestyle. Southern Appalachian Whites, Blacks, and most Indians share a similar folk existence, even though they participate in separate groups. A strong sense of family, kinship, and community, clannishness, and religiosity are characteristic of all three cultures.

Their religion also serves a folk function. In essence, these southern Appalachian churches are primary, family institutions and not public, secondary institutions as they are in the larger society. Focus is on the hereafter and not the here-and-now, as it is for many contemporary religious groups, whether they be Catholic, Protestant, or Jewish. In this sense southern Appalachian fundamentalism closely resembles medieval Catholicism in that its members are encouraged to live a humble life here on earth in exchange for everlasting salvation in the hereafter. This is not only the antithesis of the Protestant Ethic, which is the underlying theme of most contemporary religions in the United States (Catholic, Protestant, and Jewish), but also it complements the traditional aboriginal Cherokee belief system, in which the human being humbles himself or herself to the paramount forces of nature. Most students of the contemporary Cherokees would in fact question agent Donaldson's contention that little trace of the aboriginal belief system has survived among the Eastern Cherokees. Quite the contrary, they have been well integrated into Christian fundamentalism, hence well disguised from the scrutiny of outsiders.

The problem of cultural and religious integration, then, does not lie with the traditionalists, but rather with the new class of marginal Cherokees. Tourism not only opened up the Cherokees to outsiders, it absorbed much of the land through development—land once used for family agricultural endeavors. Even though the Cherokees once claimed millions of acres of territory, today they hold title only to about 56,500 acres. Much of this land consists of mountains, leaving only about 10 percent suitable for agriculture. About 7,000 enrolled Cherokees live on this land, while another 1,000 or so live adjacent to tribal trust lands. In the past this land sufficed in maintaining the Appalachian Cherokee population mainly because of cooperative agricultural endeavors. The proportion of agricultural lands, however, has diminished since the advent of the tourist industry, with only 1 percent of the land now so used.

About 30 percent of the Cherokee population has managed to retain the old traditional ways since the advent of tourism, while a small elite of less than 10 percent have been absorbed into the new "generalized American middle class." Unfortunately the remaining 60 percent are caught up in a marginal situation, with one foot in the Cherokee culture and the other in the larger dominant society. Separation of the majority of the Cherokees from the land only seems to be part of the problem. Another significant factor is the creation of the "Cherokee Myth," a promotional device designed by the federal government and private White business concerns in an attempt to promote the Cherokee as a tourist attraction.

The federal government's interest in the Cherokee increased when plans were made for the half-million-acre Great Smoky Mountain National Park. In the master plan the settlement known as Cherokee, North Carolina, was to serve as the major drawing card to the park. For this to occur it had to bolster its Indian image. This was done by two means, both of which were masterminded by Dr. Harold Foght, Cherokee agency superintendent, in conjunction with two other men. These two were Ross Caldwell, a former engineer and for many years a licensed trader in Cherokee, and Kermit Hunter, who wrote the Cherokee drama "Unto These Hills," an elaboration of Dr. Foght's original 1935 pageant based on Mooney's myths (Bauer 1970). First, a general "movie-Indian" image had to be developed for the main "tourist strip." This area includes tourist shops with "Indian artifacts" made in Japan and Korea as well as phenotypically Indian Cherokees "chiefing" in front of these shops, posing to have their pictures taken in full feathered dress for a fee.

The secondary plan was to establish a more sophisticated cultural enterprise for the more dignified tourists. This aspect included an Indian village, the Cherokee drama, and a tourist museum. Both tourist endeavors were run by Whites, with the profits going to mostly non-Indian businessmen. These White businessmen, incidentally, were not indigenous mountain folk but were valley businessmen and outsiders. One group, the Cherokee Historical Association, gained considerable federal support from the Bureau of Indian Affairs, the federal Park Service, and later from the Economic Development Administration. This group puts on the drama and maintains the tourist village and the tourist museum. Former Cherokee Vice-Chief Fred Bauer criticized these endeavors because of the psychological damage they have inflicted on a generation of Cherokees:

> The Drama has won wide acclaim as a masterful production, and rightly so. However, one must take into account the psychological effect upon the Indian over a twenty-year period. And undeniably it has had its effect. In the first place, though not historically accurate regarding the Eastern Band, it vividly portrays injustices, kindles resentment, and makes Indians storm inwardly as each new season begins. The story is carried in the press, in special editions, in magazines and brochures. If the Drama stirs audiences, how much more must it arouse Indians who live with it always? . . . Little Indian children are in the cast, and a generation has grown to adulthood impressed with the Drama as their history. Many older Indians have accepted it, not having the truth. The Myth comes at the Indians from all sides, it has completely supplanted the history, and the true origin of the Eastern Band is not to be found (Bauer 1970 : 55).

The new economy and the resulting change in the sociocultural composition of the Indian population attracted new missionaries among the Eastern Cherokees and stimulated a renewed mandate for the traditional missionaries. These changes in turn resulted in a rapid increase in churches on the reservation. While there were a dozen or so Baptist churches and one Methodist church serving the Eastern Band prior to World War II, there are 27 churches today—21 Baptist, 1 Methodist (with 3 satellites), 1 Pentecostal Holiness, 1 Church of God, 1 Episcopal, 1 Latter Day Saints (Mormon), and 1 Roman Catholic. All these churches can be classified as missionary churches. The Baptist and Pentecostal Holiness are traditional fundamentalist churches, while the Methodist and Church of God are neofundamentalists (the difference here being that the neofundamentalists use ordained ministers, while the traditional fundamentalists utilize lay preachers). The three nonfundamentalist churches—Episcopal, Mormon, and Catholic—maintain their respective traditional religious services among their Cherokee congregations.

Renewed competition has emerged between the fundamentalist churches, each vying for its share of the traditional and marginal Cherokee population. The changing Cherokee lifestyle even led to divisiveness among the Baptists themselves. The increasing marginal population no longer felt welcome at the traditional Baptist churches, leading to the emergence of new Baptist churches to serve this group. A major factor distinguishing the traditionalist from the marginal Cherokee congregation is the use of the Cherokee language in the church service. This divisiveness also affected the reservation's sole Methodist church. Early in this process of socioeconomic change among the Eastern Cherokees, the Blue Wing Methodist Church split, giving rise to two new congregations—the Pentecostal Holiness and the Church of God.

The more conventional denominations became firmly established as late as the mid-1960's, serving only a small proportion of the population, the White and Indian middle class. Prior to the establishment of their Cherokee congregations, the Whites on the reservation, mainly bureaucrats and businessmen, had to attend church services in nearby White communities. However, two factors seemed to contribute to the development of these "higher" denomination churches on the reservation itself. One factor was the creation of a new, visible, yet small Cherokee middle class.

The other factor was the passage of the 1964 Civil Rights Act. The Mormons best illustrate this. The Latter Day Saints came under fire following the enactment of the Civil Rights Act, with their critics asserting that the church actively discriminated against nonwhites. Many feel that the Mormons, being torn between accepting all nonwhites or selecting a particular racial minority, chose Indians as evidence of their attempt to comply with the Civil Rights Act. Since 1964, American Indians have been actively sought for membership. A consequence of this effort is that a large proportion of Native Americans attend Brigham Young University, the private Mormon school. American Indians are known as "Lamenites" by the Mormons. They believe that American Indians represent one of the lost tribes of Israel. While the Cherokee Mormon branch president is White, as are half of the 120-member congregation, both of the branch counselors are enrolled Cherokees. Moreover, both counselors are successful Cherokee businessmen, one being the president of the Cherokee Chamber of Commerce.

The other middle-class Cherokees are mostly either Episcopalian or Catholic. Among the other congregations, only the Baptists have Cherokee preachers. Most of these lay preachers give their sermons in the native language and serve congregations comprised of traditional Indians.

In summation, a dual religious ideology seems to have evolved among the Eastern Cherokees. On the one hand Protestant fundamentalism emerged as the traditional Christian belief system for the bulk of the Indians, while contemporary Protestantism and Catholicism, those religious sects supportive of the Protestant Ethic, have more recently made inroads into the Cherokee culture, serving the small elite of middle-class Indians. Although both ideological systems are Christian, they are basically contravening in nature. Fundamentalism is supportive of the "accommodative reservation" survival system as well as of the old traditional Indian cultural lifestyle. The Protestant Ethic and the new nonfundamentalist religions, on the other hand, represent the dominant society and its regulatory forces among the Eastern Cherokees.

A recent statement by Kermit Hunter, author of "Unto These Hills," perhaps best illustrates a common ethnocentric interpretation of the Indian culture and the role of religion in regulating these people: "The best Indian is a white Indian, the whiter the better. . . . They had nothing until the white missionaries got hold of them, taught them to read and write, fed them, clothed them. . . . Everything the Indian has learned, he learned through white blood" (Oppy 1976).

Hunter's statement hints at the recent controversies emerging on the Qualla Boundary Reservation, resulting in the polarization of the tribe into two camps, the middle class and traditionalist. Both these parties actively solicit support from the large, heretofore ignored, marginal class. The new underground tribal newspaper *The Cherokee Wildfire* is evidence of this new movement toward traditionalism and cultural self-determination. As might be expected, the best indicator of these contravening social groups is their religious affiliation. Those Cherokees belonging to the conventional denominations are often labeled as being part of the small middle-class elite and therefore linked to the dominant control apparatus, which now is coming under increased criticism by the traditionalists.

Not only is the reservation system being attacked by the traditionalists for its alleged neglect of the "real Indian," but also the entire tourist industry network is being attacked for similar reasons. Essentially, the traditionalists are questioning the larger issue of federal paternalism and adolescent accommodation. They feel that many of those who claim to speak for the Cherokees are in actuality serving their own self-interest and not that of the tribe. Consequently, successful middle-class Cherokees, those who belong to the more conventional churches (Mormon, Catholic, and Episcopal), are often linked with these "exploitative" agencies (BIA, Cherokee Historical Association, Cherokee Chamber of Commerce) regardless of whether they are associated with the agencies or not.

As a result of these shifts, now both inter- and intraethnic communications are following religious lines. While any attempt to anticipate the results of this current controversy among the Qualla Cherokees would merely be conjectural, tribal council elections could in the near future establish a direction in this social movement. Surely these events challenge the assumption of Gulick (1960) and others that the Cherokees were at the "cross roads of assimilation" nearly three decades ago.

I have attempted to demonstrate here the interface of religious groups with traditional tribal society and to explore the ways in which religion becomes a means of adapting to or resisting change. In developing this line of thought I have called on Goffman's model of total institutions to explain in part the structure of action between controllers (BIA, government agencies) and the controlled population (reservation Indians). In this interaction the churches become either instruments of control or, conversely, instruments for resistance and cultural continuity.

REFERENCES

Bauer, Fred B., 1970. *Land of the North Carolina Cherokees* (Brevard, N.C.: Buchanan Press).

Bruce, Dickson, 1974. *And They All Sang Hallelujah* (Knoxville: University of Tennessee Press).

Collier, Peter, 1973. *When Shall They Rest?* (New York: Holt, Rinehart and Winston).

Donaldson, Thomas, 1892. *Extra Census Bulletin* (Washington, D.C.: Government Printing Office).

Goffman, Erving, 1961. *Asylums* (Garden City, N.Y.: Anchor Books).

Gulick, John, 1960. *Cherokees at the Crossroads* (Chapel Hill: University of North Carolina Press).

Gusfield, Joseph, 1963. *Symbolic Crusade* (Chicago: University of Chicago Press).

Malone, Henry T., 1956. *Cherokees of the Old South* (Athens: University of Georgia Press).

Mooney, James, 1972. *Myths of the Cherokees and Sacred Formulas of the Cherokees* (Nashville: Charles Elder) (reprinted).

Reid, John, 1970. *A Law of Blood* (New York: New York University Press).

Snook, John B., 1973. *Going Further* (Englewood Cliffs, N.J.: Prentice-Hall).

Thomas, Robert K., 1958. *Eastern Cherokee Acculturation* (M.A. thesis, University of North Carolina).

Oppy, Jane, 1976. "A Racist at Large," *Wassajae*, 4 (11 and 12): 10.

Ethnic Nationalism and Political Mobilization in Industrial Societies

RICHARD G. FOX, CHARLOTTE AULL, LOUIS CIMINO

Partly motivated by the desire to confront the many social problems that beset contemporary societies and partly driven by the necessity to move the discipline beyond the fast-disappearing primitive and peasant world, anthropologists have increasingly addressed research problems on ethnicity in complex societies. Anthropologists generally agree that ethnicity refers to self-conscious populations bounded from the majority or from each other by imposed or self-imposed genealogical, historical, religious, linguistic, or other cultural "diacritica" (see Barth 1969), although they may disagree about whether these diacritica are "primordial" or "situational" (see Keyes 1976). From this definition, anthropologists have gone on to analyze the adaptive or acculturative roles followed by specific ethnic groups or the nature of interethnic relations and identities regulating social boundaries (see Gans 1962; Tomasi and Engel 1970; Cronin 1970; Hannerz 1974; Stack 1974; Nagata 1974). In this literature ethnicity from a general interest in political mobilization and in the and the anthropologist focuses on the way ethnicity is retained or lost or on the ways ethnicity is situationally manipulated by individuals and populations.

Our current research project treats ethnicity in a rather different manner and addresses research questions at some remove from either the acculturation or the boundary viewpoints.[1] We approach the study of ethnicity from a general interest in political mobilization and in the changing patterns of integration found in complex societies (for a similar approach, see Barnett 1974; Brass 1976; Enloe 1973). We therefore conceive of ethnicity as a dependent variable, as a by-product of particular social institutions and political circumstances in the wider society. Specifically, our interest lies in social situations where ethnicity acts as a political ideology that may be manipulated by elites and as a social institution that underlies new forms of political association in industrial societies. The particular content of ethnicity or the affectual and social boundaries it supports do not enter directly into this analysis. Our major questions are not what ethnicity leads or permits individuals or groups to do or how it defines what they are (in a cultural sense), but rather under what social situations ethnic allegiances and ideologies form the basis of political mobilization and how such ethnically mobilized populations are thereby fitted into the political context of the wider society. Specifically, our work focuses on the nature of industrial societies in which a particular form of political mobilization, which we call ethnic nationalism, has recently taken place, on the role played by sophisticated ethnic leaders in creating such movements, on the reconstituted or newly created ideologies espoused by such leaders for political mobilization, and on the way in which such ethnic nationalisms reformulate or attempt to reformulate political institutions within such industrial societies.

ETHNIC NATIONALISM

Ethnic nationalism can be defined as the occurrence in a modernized society of political or quasi-political groups whose organizing principle, mobilization of adherents, and appeals for redress of presumed inequities are based on ethnic identity. Ethnic nationalism is a pervasive factor in many industrial societies and one that scholars sometimes portray as an atavism of ethnic identities not fully extinguished, as a refractory plaque on the construction of unified politics (see Enloe 1973 for criticism of this position). However, the ubiquitous quality of ethnic nationalisms— the Acadian revival and Quebec separatist movement in Canada; the black liberation, Cajun revival, and Amerindian movement in the United States; the Welsh and Scottish nationalist agitation in Great Britain; the Samish movement in Norway; the Breton, Corsican, Occitanic, and Alsatian autonomists in France; the Flamande-Walloon confrontation in Belgium; and the Basque terrorism in Spain—belies explaining these nationalisms as survivals that continue due to their own (ethnic) inertia. To be sure, populations that evidence ethnic nationalism have generally had a long-standing minority position within the larger society, and the regions they inhabit may have in the past constituted internal colonies (see Wolpe 1975). To portray ethnic nationalism as arising solely from these historic connections ignores the dynamic aspects of such ethnicity, the novel political mobilization that it attempts, and the significant role of ethnic elites in its genesis.

We present below a brief discussion of three approaches to ethnic nationalism that our research over the last two years seriously questions. The discussion is then followed by an alternative theoretical statement about ethnic nationalism, its genesis and development. The concluding section presents case materials from the Acadian ethnic nationalist movement to support our position.

Our research seriously questions the validity of explanations or descriptions of political mobilization carried out by ethnic nationalist movements as (*a*) breakdowns in modernization, (*b*) responses to internal colonialism, or (*c*) "past-oriented," conservative social movements (as distinct from "future-oriented," radical class movements).

Breakdowns in Modernization. The concept of breakdowns in modernization was proposed by S. N. Eisenstadt (1964) to explain the recursion of partially modernized new nations to more traditional, particularistic, and ascriptive patterns of social and political organization. Eisenstadt suggests that the rapid economic and political mobilization experienced by these states could not be institutionalized within modernized forms and therefore led to a partial reinstatement of a traditional order—even though this traditional order contained new ascriptive or quasi-ascriptive loyalties and identities mobilized by the incomplete modernization process. As applied to ethnic national movements in industrial societies, this concept would propose that the modernization and centralization of industrial nation-states over the last century has brought forth a backlash of primordial ethnic sentiment, regional identities, and by extension, ethnic political opposition. The major problem with this explanation, as with much of the modernization literature, is its assumption that certain identities and institutions, like ethnicity, are less modernized than others, such as the bureaucratic nation-state. The ethnic constituency mobilized by such nationalist movements then becomes simply an eruption of (dormant? primordial?) regional or group sentiments that were not fully eradicated by the encroaching nation-state and its modernized institutions.

Our analysis casts doubt on the interpretation of ethnic nationalism as a breakdown in modernization in two respects. First, ethnic nationalist movements are organized around the political and social institutions of the modernized nation-state. Whether in legal proceedings, political party opposition and electoral contests, or simply as pressure groups (sometimes violent ones), ethnic nationalist movements do not utilize traditional structures to pursue their goals. Their ideology may be personalistic (but no more so than the nation-state's call for allegiance to flag and family), but their structure is universalistic. Rather than a primordial allegiance that springs up into an organized political movement, we believe that ethnic nationalisms are better explained as political movements that simply utilize a presumed shared ethnicity—as other political movements use assumed common economic class status—as their basis for recruitment (compare van den Berghe, n.d.).

This assertion is buttressed by our second demurrer to the breakdown-in-modernization interpretation. In many respects, the ethnicity utilized as a basis for recruitment and allegiance by these movements is a reconstituted one, especially among the movements' leaders. Thus, many Basque and Welsh leaders did not know the languages upon which they based their regional protest but purposely learned them to further their political ends. Acadian leaders all speak French, but a highly refined and grammatical version that bears little relationship to the Canadian French dialect spoken by their uneducated followers. This situation appears also among the Lapps and Bretons. Other symbols that presently rationalize ethnic nationalisms—the history of economic exploitation, famous past martyrs for the cause—are often equally recent creations or have only assumed importance as leaders have reconstituted them for a mass audience. Rather than a primordial loyalty that suddenly gains political embodiment, this neo-ethnicity may be affirmed precisely to build a political movement. The important question then becomes not: What led to a breakdown in the nation-state? (as modernization theorists ask), but rather: Out of what political conditions does a movement based on ethnicity grow and hope to exploit? To answer this question, the focus must shift from the national-level concerns (and bias) of the modernization theorist to the organization, leadership, and ideology of these nationalist movements—a change in focus that leads us to answer the above questions along lines suggested later in this study.

Internal Colonialism. Ethnic nationalist movements have increasingly been explained as protests against "internal colonialism." Hechter, for example, has argued that differential industrialization and an ethnic division of labor in Great Britain has led disadvantaged regions (Scotland and Wales) to political protests against their inequality within the industrial nation-state (Hechter 1971, 1975).

Several limitations seriously indict the utility of this explanation, not the least of which is the failure of its proponents to specify clearly the constituent features or defining characteristics of internal colonialism (Hechter 1975:33 n.l).[2] As a result this term often serves simply as a descriptive and pejorative label, rather than an analytic concept of any power. Indeed, the internal-colonialism argument often appears to be simply a scholarly formulation of ideological elements espoused by many ethnic nationalist movements, a strange but hardly unique case of the *emic* being converted into the scholarly *etic* (see Sahlins 1976 for an equivalent argument about sociobiology).

An equally serious limitation is the inability of the internal-colonialism argument to specify why nationalist movements have only recently assumed political or quasi-political forms and generated successful mass appeals. Given Hechter's analysis, Scotland and Wales were internal colonies by 1850 (if not much earlier), yet their nationalist movements achieved popular recognition and electoral success only after 1960. The same hiatus between onset of internal colonialism and development of ethnic nationalism occurs in Brittany (Berger n.d.), Acadian New Brunswick, among American Indians, and the Lapps. This relationship between former internal colonialism and present nationalist movement is made even more moot by the fact that the recent genesis of such movements coincides with increased state welfare and social expenditures in such regions, which ostensibly lessens rather than heightens their inferior status (we return to this point below). Furthermore, economic deprivation, whether past or present, cannot explain why the middle-class and well-educated ethnics whom we have found to lead these movements choose to pursue regional development and to build ethnic solidarity.

Finally, the internal-colonialism argument cannot effectively predict where ethnic nationalist movements will arise and prosper. Puerto Rico has been an internal colony of the United States for almost a century, but the nationalist movements have generally been weak and increasingly unpopular. Conversely, the Spanish Basque region, locale for one of the most potent nationalist movements, is also the center of the greatest industrialization and wealth in the society (Douglass and da Silva 1971). Similarly, Alsace is not an economically or industrially underprivileged area, yet the demands for autonomy and the ethnic allegiance that underlie nationalist movements are increasingly found in this region of France. Even under the loosest definition, therefore, internal colonialism appears to be neither a sufficient nor necessary condition for the genesis of an ethnic nationalist movement.

Ethnicity as Past-Oriented. In a recent book an ethnic identity, De Vos characterizes ethnicity as oriented to the past, whereas he sees class consciousness as future-oriented (DeVos 1975). The former is reactionary and conserving; the latter is radical and innovative. Under this interpretation, ethnic nationalisms would appear as a series of attempts to redress the present in the values of the past, an assertion of the important status of cultural "things" in a national political and economic order based on contract and commodity. However, this contrast between ethnic and class identities does not effectively characterize many ethnic nationalist movements. Although in their earliest stages they were often primarily cultural and therefore conserving and past-oriented, the Welsh, Scottish, Basque, Breton, and Acadian movements (or elements of them) now espouse radical economic and political demands that call for rectification of presumed past inequalities and require plans for future development. These protests impute a common status of inequality or disfranchisement to the region or ethnic population as a whole, and therefore ethnic identity is used to mobilize attempts (sometimes legal, often political, occasionally violent) at reordering of the nation-state. To differentiate class consciousness from ethnic identity, as DeVos proposes, may miss this very important incorporation of classlike political and economic conflicts as essential mobilizing, or organizing, factors in these movements—and thereby may fail to specify the conditions under which such incorporation takes place and its significance in the explanation of these movements.

The three explanations of ethnic nationalism discussed above have proved to be of limited utility as our research has progressed. The following paragraphs outline an alternative explanation of these movements that has emerged from our work.

ETHNIC NATIONALISMS AS NOVEL POLITICAL FORMS

Ethnic nationalisms can best be explained, we believe, as new organizational forms for political and economic protest that occur in industrial societies as an alternative to and replacement for class-based forms of social protest. They occur therefore in societal situations where class politics and protest have not developed or where they no longer effectively mobilize political action. The salient characteristic of ethnic nationalism is its ability (or attempt) to bind local populations differentiated by class, age, sex, education, and residence into a united political front seeking redress from the central government. The appeal to ethnicity and the cultural diacritica like language, religion, and history that symbolize it may provide an effective base for political mobilization that overcomes the separate and antagonistic loyalties, allegiances, and even class organization separating urban from rural, middle class from lower class.

The history of industrial nations over the last century, but especially since World War II, represents a steadily decreasing distinction between urban and rural lifeways and a diminution of economic class conflict, as the ever more powerful welfare state steadily intrudes bureaucratic regulation into all aspects of economic, political, and social life (see Gouldner 1970 : 349–350). Political mobilization on the basis of class opposition, of right versus left, becomes less potent and is replaced by appeals to presumed or asserted shared cultural diacritica—ethnicity, sex, community—in motivating mass political activity. Rather than breakdowns in modernization or backward-looking ideologies, ethnic nationalisms are therefore political and social responses to the new power arrangements in highly bureaucratic (welfare) states and attempts at political mobilization to lobby with the state. They represent responses to the furthest development of the nation-state, and in form, action, and ideology they reflect novel social movements unlike either the proletarian radicalism of nineteenth-century industrial societies or the rural fascism of the twentieth.[3]

Ethnic nationalism is therefore one kind of locality or local-level response to government intrusion in a political system where government controls the major power sources and where policies are legislated and implemented by the center with great consequences for the local level (Reiter 1972). For the locality or population to organize an effective protest, it must bridge urban-rural, cultural, economic, age, and sex divisions, and must supplant class consciousness, if it has been organized, with other consciousness. Ethnicity—to the extent it can be ideologically created or reinvigorated, but in any case redefined by a self-conscious elite in a new (political) context and for novel ends (directed against the central government)—is an obvious choice.

The ideologies espoused by many nationalist movements are good clues to the problems of organization and the nature of the protest movements they represent:

1. A common motif is to decry the degree of bureaucratic centralization and the loss of local autonomy in political, economic, and social decision making. Such a motif characterizes not only presumed internal colonies like Wales but also highly privileged locales like the Basque region and Alsace.

2. A variant of the above is the assertion that the individual has been dehumanized in the modern industrial state and turned into a code number on a bureaucratic ledger. This ideology asserts an equality of individuals—if only in the sense that they are all equally stripped and ciphered—that ignores differences of age, sex, rural-urban provenience, and economic status within the ethnic population.

3. A strong motif is the assertion that because they are Welshmen (or Breton, or whatever), all Welsh are equal. The importance of affirming the cultural heritage—whether in terms of language, religion, or history—is that given their common possession of these diacritica, they can all be said to be equal.

4. Another common theme is that of internal colonialism (although perhaps not labeled such) and a history of exploitation by the majority. This motif again asserts equality among the ethnic population, in this case an equality founded on common external exploitation.

5. Especially in Europe, a strong ideological current in ethnic nationalist movements concerns the necessity of a world or continental political

or economic regime rather than a nationalist one. Centralization is to be feared only in the form of the oppressive nation-state, again another way of mobilizing resistance to the incursive welfare/bureaucratic regime.

This explanation of ethnic nationalist movements underlines the importance of leaders from within the ethnic population for the genesis and development of such movements. The common scholarly treatment of ethnic collectivities or aggregates as unstratified or undifferentiated populations obscures the hypothesized fact that the leaders of ethnic nationalisms are often highly acculturated middle-class professionals who reconstitute their ethnicity and broadcast new symbols of identity and forms of organization to an ethnic following. To the extent that this leadership or elite can create an ideology and organization that bridges urban-rural differences; that links the ethnic aggregate even though some are wealthier, better educated, and more powerful than others; and that supersedes class bases of political organization (should such exist), nationalist movements are set in motion.

Ethnic nationalist movements develop, we believe, in five phases:

The *incipient phase* is characterized by the existence of an inchoate ethnic population, or collectivity, sharing a diffuse ethnic identity and sometimes but not always an inferior economic and political situation in the society. This collectivity may inhabit a contiguous ethnic homeland or may be widely distributed throughout the society, and the degree of territorial nucleation may have important consequences for the ethnic identity felt. However, the ethnic population is not organized around institutions or articulated common symbols, and there is no ethnic elite.

The *formative phase* sees the development of an ethnic elite that organizes into associations, clubs, societies, and other voluntary groups on the basis of shared ethnicity. In the early formative phase, these associations bind together elites at a fairly local level; in the later formative phase, provincial or national associations are developed that define an ethnic elite of much wider compass. This ethnic elite is usually drawn from the most acculturated of the ethnic population, that is, those who are able situationally to dispose of the ethnic markers or diacritica most effectively.

Such ethnic elites are thrown up to act as brokers in the interstices between the bureaucratic nation-state and the local and regional community, either because they develop skills needed by the nation-state as a result of their acculturation or because they claim to represent their ethnic congeners. During this phase, however, ethnic nationalisms are in no sense mass movements. Their associational activities are organized and enjoyed by the elite, and the latter make few attempts to mobilize an ethnic following in actuality. Over the course of the formative phase, the associations created by the ethnic elite often become more secular and the ideology of ethnic mobilization also takes on a more secular, and therefore more directly political, cast.

The next phase, the *florescent*, has generally occurred in Western industrial nation-states in the wake of World War II and the bureaucratic and technological capabilities it brought such states. The ensuing welfare state assumes responsibility for health, welfare, economic planning, environmental services, transportation and communication, education, sociocultural activities—services previously performed by local civic organizations and private associations and institutions (including ethnic or ethnically based ones) or not previously performed.

The heightened intrusion of welfare-state administration and control threatens the ethnic elite's privileged position or its intermediary role between government and locality that existed in the formative phase. It may also threaten the elite's position within the ethnic population by coopting the services previously offered through the ethnic association. To protect their own positions with respect to the government and within the ethnic population, the elite recognize that they must deal aggressively with the state. In the absence of functional political groups such as labor unions and in the absence of electoral institutions that properly represent ethnic needs, the elite turn to political pressure to guarantee their continued privilege. To apply such pressure effectively, however, they must mobilize the ethnic population to a hitherto unknown extent, since the ethnic population is the only guarantee of state willingness to listen. This mobilization sets in motion developments that the ethnic elite often do not foresee and sometimes cannot control. For instance, the ideology of ethnic nationalist movements in the florescent phase usually takes on a more radical tone. More importantly, the new mobilization throws up new contenders for elite position, often younger and more radical, who may threaten or even successfully challenge the older elite's position or who may push the movement to acts of subversion or violence.

The *matured phase* is simply a continuation and further development of the mobilization and politicization of the ethnic population begun in the florescent phase. Political opposition becomes more direct and public. Depending on the political framework of the society and the historical pattern that linked the ethnic collectivity to the wider society, this direct, public political action may take the form of ethnic party politics, legal proceedings, mass political sabotage, mass ethnic cultural performances, or a combination of these.

The approach to ethnic nationalism outlined above derives from secondary research on many of these movements and primary research in Wales and Acadia (Francophone New Brunswick). Space allows only the most cursory review of the developmental pattern in the latter area as illustration of the general points made above.

ACADIAN ETHNIC NATIONALISM

Acadian ethnic nationalism is a recent phenomenon and has not progressed beyond the florescent phase.

Incipient Phase. The Acadians (Francophones) of New Brunswick, one of the Canadian Maritime Provinces, are the descendants of the early French colony of Acadie. After originally expelling the French speakers in 1755, the British allowed them to return (or come out of hiding) in 1763. However, Acadian nationalism has its roots in the mid- to late nineteenth century. In 1860 the Acadians represented less than 15 percent of the New Brunswick population (Roy 1976)[4] and were concentrated along the eastern and northern borders of the province. Several scholars characterize Acadian society in 1860 as minimally organized, without economic or political contact with the wider society. Thorburn, for example, writes:

> During the century after the expulsion, the Acadians lived in New Brunswick; yet they played virtually no part in the life of the community. Communications were so poor that many had no contact with the English-speaking communities during their entire lives. As Catholics they were excluded from politics by the requirement of an oath of non-belief in transubstantiation. . . . As a result there were virtually no Acadians in commerce or industry, and practically none with either capital or learning; they lived apart by farming and fishing. (1961 : 23; for other descriptions of Acadian society at the time see Baudry 1966; Mailhot 1973, 1976; Rumilly 1955 : 654–715)

Formative Phase (early). Between 1860 and 1920 the French Catholic church emerged as the premier institution of Acadian society in the context of Acadian political impotency and economic stagnation within the wider society. The founding of College St. Joseph at Memramcook, New Brunswick, in 1864 by a French-Canadian priest, Père Camille Lefebvre, represents the single most important event for the subsequent development of Acadian nationalism. The college recruited and developed an Acadian elite consisting mainly of clerics, but including lay professionals, lawyers, doctors, and teachers.

The French-speaking priests, assigned to various parishes in the Acadian sector, emerged as local leaders because they were often the only educated individuals in the village. They attended to two major problems: the lack of education and the penetration of the Acadian subsistence economy by external capitalist enterprises in the fishing and timber trades (see Doucet 1973 : 89–188 for the activities of the priest, and Mailhot 1973, 1976, for a detailed economic analysis). They never cured the malaise stemming from these two conditions, but their proposed solutions, utilizing religious institutions and religious ideology, became the basis of Acadian nationalistic endeavor.

In 1880, sixteen years after the foundation of College St. Joseph, Acadian leaders from all parts of the Maritimes came together as a single group for the first time at the National Congress of the St. Jean Baptiste Society in Quebec. This convention is the first evidence for the formation of supralocal elite institutions, but a more firmly grounded elite institutional structure was to follow. A separate Acadian convention for Memramcook was organized the following year. That convention and others following it codified Acadian nationalist ideology.[5] The French clergy dominated the conventions even if laymen led them. They were exofficio delegates and often presided over the study groups. Their ideology can be summarized as follows:

Acadian society is initially depicted as a rural utopia. Harmonious agricultural communities, carved from virgin forests, enjoy the bounties of nature. The ancestors are lauded for their religiosity, gentility, pioneering spirit, perseverance, and humility. The expulsion by the British, Le Grand Dérangement, abruptly ends this golden age. A century of misery and untold hardship follows, during which the Acadians represented a martyred people, tenaciously clinging to their faith and their language, *la plus belle langue du monde*. Emulation of the ancestors is the proposed means of restoring Acadian society to its original condition. Acadians must be devoted to their religion, best sustained by keeping the French language. They must be committed to education to produce the priests, doctors, lawyers, and merchants the new Acadian society will need. Finally, they must return to the original economic patterns of their ancestors, agriculture. If these were to be done a united French, and Catholic, Acadie would emerge from the abyss into which Acadian society has fallen. In further elaborations of the ideology, this last phase is termed La Renaissance (see Robidoux 1907 for ideology and Hautecoeur 1975 for analysis).

Formative Phase (late). Acadian nationalism had progressed considerably by 1900, as evidenced by the appearance of two newspapers and two new colleges. Sixty Acadian priests, their numbers buttressed by many more from Quebec, were active in the Maritimes. They attracted a number of religious communities, and major convents had been established. A patriotic organization, Société de l'Assomption, organized major congresses from time to time.

Because of its overtly religious motif and emphasis on indigenous development, Acadian nationalism did not threaten the New Brunswick political establishment, but it severely threatened the Irish-dominated ecclesiastical establishment. Since the 1880's the English-speaking bishops had grown increasingly alarmed at the deepening Acadian consciousness, particularly the link forged between religion and faith. Not surprisingly, the relations between the prelates and the French-speaking priests deteriorated (Doucet 1973). An ecclesiastical fight for control of the diocese in the Acadian sector was inevitable.

The bitter struggle consumed the first two decades of this century (Doucet 1973 : 201–242; Rumilly 1955 : 915–17; Savoie 1976 : 83–98). By 1920 Acadians controlled both the diocese and a new parish in Moncton, which in 1936 became the center of a new ecclesiastical province with an Acadian archbishop; thus Acadians gained complete control over the Catholic church, and the Acadian elite enjoyed a permanent institutional structure at a supralocal level.

Between 1920 and 1960 the Acadian leadership and other institutions became firmly grounded around this ecclesiastical structure. The ideology was elaborated to the point where there existed no distinction between "French" and "Catholic." La Société de l'Assomption Mutuelle (not to be confused with the patriotic society mentioned above) developed as a fraternal mutual aid society through a network of lodges. The clergy enthusiastically supported membership in the society, which became a focal point of village life. The society set up a special scholarship fund to send students to the classical colleges. The church also supported the Caisses Populaires (credit unions) springing up after 1936 because no other savings institutions existed then. Both these organizations have become major financial institutions and both represent implementations of the ideology emphasizing indigenous development under the guidance of the church. These organizations represent the earliest economic and political mobilization of the Acadian population by the ethnic elite.

At the local level the priest remained the most prominent leader in the village, followed in prestige by the doctor, lawyer, and male teachers. A village would most likely have a small convent and nuns engaged in teaching, hospital services, and domestic services for the priests. Teaching brothers established schools in some of the larger settlements, but they were never as ubiquitous as the nuns or priests. In the eyes of the local population, the church—not the municipal authorities or the representatives of the provincial authorities—provided basic education and health services.

At both the local and pan-Acadian levels the Catholic church consolidated its hold on Acadian society. It predominated because the system of provincial-municipal relations created in the 1870's vested important fiscal and administrative responsibility in local county governments and school districts (Whalen 1963 : 11–38). In the Acadian sector the Catholic church assumed responsibilities that should have been discharged by local school districts or the county municipalities because the only effective local social organization then in existence was entirely a product of the parish structure of the Catholic church. The "civic structures" created and recognized by the province existed in name only.

The Catholic church had been the first locus of Acadian nationalist struggle precisely because it was a powerful institution that controlled education, provided "welfare" and health services, and formed the structure of local leadership. The church maintained its position because of the poverty in the Acadian sector (see Mailhot 1973, 1976, for a discussion of its historical basis and Even 1970, for a summary description in the mid-1960's). The municipalities never had the resources to provide services without dependence upon those of the church—its organizational capacity and its supply of "cheap labor" in the form of nuns who were active in education and health services. Table 1 compares the fiscal capacity of English and French county municipalities; clearly the Acadians are in a very inferior economic position.

Florescent Phase. The church maintained its integral position until the early 1960's, but the factors bringing about its decline were set in motion before then. As the 1950's progressed, financing of education became increasingly burdensome for all New Brunswick municipalities, but especially for the Acadian sector—even with substantial church subsidy. Provincial education grants were available, but most were based on a per capita or percentage-of-cost basis and therefore could not equalize the growing economic disparity resulting from uneven urbanization and industrialization. In 1955 a royal commission on school finance recommended greater provincial participation in financing education by making the equalization principle the basis of provincial grants. The Association Acadienne d'Education, a church-related education service organization, repeatedly sought greater provincial participation in the late 1950's even though fifteen years earlier it resisted provincial attempts to promote high school construction. By 1960 most New Brunswick political observers clearly saw that the province would have to share a greater percentage not only of education costs, but of costs for other social services as well (Whalen 1963 : 59ff.).

New Brunswick politics received a jolt in 1960 when Louis J. Robichaud was elected the first Acadian premier. Perhaps the most charismatic New Brunswick politician of the century, Robichaud won the election on the strength of personality and political acumen. Neither

Table 1. Actual property tax assessments per capita,
converted to estimated full market value,
county municipalities of New Brunswick, 1962.

County	Percentage of French origin*	Percentage of total population of French origin	Per capita value of property (Canadian dollars)	Percent of mean
Albert	3.2	0.2	2,164	164
Carleton	3.5	0.4	1,088	83
Kings	3.6	0.4	2,119	161
York	6.3	1.4	2,520	191
Charlotte	6.4	0.6	1,055	80
Queens	8.5	0.4	1,253	95
St. John	13.8	5.3	2,179	165
Sunbury	17.3	1.7	902	68
Northumberland	31.4	6.8	510	39
Victoria	42.3	3.6	2,021	153
Westmorland	43.7	17.6	1,515	115
Restigouche	68.3	12.1	651	49
Kent	82.0	9.4	414	31
Gloucester	85.2	24.3	447	34
Madawaska	93.8	15.8	925	70
Mean	38.8 (weighted)		1,317	

Source: Part of Table 7 : 1, New Brunswick (1963), p. 115.
* From the 1961 census. Percentage of the entire population of county including incorporated urban municipalities. Census does not break down ethnic origin beyond the county level for incorporated units less than 10,000.

ethnicity nor Acadian rights were mentioned in the campaign. But Robichaud was also a member in good standing of the Acadian establishment. He had been a member of the AAE and wrote a major detailed brief on the economic plight of Acadian schools. Coming from Kent County, he understood the economic hardship of the French and some rural English counties and determined that the province would help. He appointed a royal commission to investigate provincial-municipal relations and propose solutions. The commission's report, from which Table 1 is taken, recommended a drastic overhaul of municipal government and the elimination of all county-level municipalities. The commission argued that education, health, welfare, and the administration of justice have a beneficial effect for the entire province and therefore are general services for which the province should assume complete financial and administrative responsibility. The commission further reasoned that only at the provincial level could a competent bureaucracy be formed. A uniform province-wide property tax based on real market value was the cornerstone of the commission's program. Considerable opposition to this program as drawn up by the Robichaud government existed, but none of it was expressed on an ethnic basis even though the Acadian sector was the most obvious beneficiary. In 1967 the legislative package was proclaimed provincial law.

The Robichaud government moved on a number of other fronts to improve the quality of life in backward areas. In 1963 the government established Université de Moncton, to which the three classical colleges then in existence in New Brunswick were affiliated. In 1966 the province entered into a substantial agreement with the federal government to develop northeastern New Brunswick (overwhelmingly French). Known as FRED, the Fund for Rural Economic Development poured approximately sixty-seven million dollars into the area by 1972 (Canada, Department of Forestry and Rural Development 1966; Canada, Department of Regional Economic Expansion 1972). The money went into the construction of schools, technical and vocational training, and infrastructural development. In 1967 the province embarked upon an ambitious school construction program in addition to the schools built with FRED funds. In 1968 the Robichaud government passed the Official Languages Act, modeled after the Federal Act, which committed the government to providing services in both official languages.

Although the Acadian elite took satisfaction in the Robichaud reforms, this intrusive provincial welfare program threatened to preempt the primary status of the church and to undercut the elite's authority. For almost one hundred years the church had maintained a financially shaky but still French Catholic school system. Robichaud replaced that with secular schools, an expanded educational bureaucracy, and a professional teaching corps, trained after 1968 at a French teacher's college. For exactly ninety-nine years the church had exclusive control over higher education; Robichaud replaced that with a provincially funded university. The church expressed interest in economic development by strong moral support of the Assumption and Caisses Populaires. The FRED program towered over their financial abilities to make improvements. Robichaud had accomplished much of what the Acadian elite wanted done but only by making the province rather than the church the responsible agent and, in the process, making the elite realize they would have to bargain aggressively within the political structure if they wished to guarantee their positions.

The late 1960's witnessed a number of events that culminated in the formation of the Société des Acadiens du Nouveau-Brunswick (SANB) in 1973. The province's ambitious school program, coupled with its assumption of complete financial responsibility, directed elite ethnic pressure onto the provincial bureaucracy.

Pressures mounted over concerns such as the location of a school or the budget for the school boards. Often they were articulated by the social activists who were in the employ of the government as *animateurs* (similar to community workers in the United States) for the FRED program or they were expressed by teachers. At the French university, students demanded higher levels of provincial support. The Moncton area school board experienced major difficulties in 1968–1970 when the francophones demanded a separate French district. By 1970 it was clear to everyone, the education minister in particular, that since the province was in complete control only concerted political action at the provincial level would achieve desired results.

The Hatfield government came to power in 1970. Younger Acadian leaders sensed the need for a special Acadian political organization for the expression of Acadian needs to the provincial authorities. They strongly distrusted the traditional electoral political system, which effectively excluded the Acadians from the political process for two centuries. Acadians never were represented in proportion to their percentage of the total population in the provincial legislature. From 1874 through 1960 the difference between the percentage of seats held by persons with French surnames and the percentage of the total population that was of French origin ranged from a low of -5.4 to -17.1 (derived from Canadian Parliamentary Guide for election years, 1870–1960). In the Cabinet, where provincial policy is formed, Acadians were even more severely underrepresented. Of the seventy-nine Cabinet ministers who held office between 1900 and 1958 only fourteen (17.7 percent) have French surnames, while the French origin population for those years (1901–61) rose from 24.2 percent to 38.8 percent. The relative paucity of Cabinet appointments also indicates Acadian impuissance in either political party (Thornburn 1961 : 204–205).

The major Acadian organization, Société Nationale des Acadiens (SNA), a direct descendant of the patriotic society that organized the first conventions, was controlled by the traditional Acadian elite. The SNA contained Acadians from all three Maritime provinces. The younger Acadians recognized this as an obsolete structure. What was needed was a strong, politically oriented organization at the provincial level.

During the same period the federal government launched the bilingualism-biculturalism (later multiculturalism) program as a response to the political tremors emanating from Quebec. The program committed the federal government to support official language minorities and their organizations in the ten provinces. This program has at least partially funded the SNA since 1969. The federal government preferred to deal with provincially based organizations. By 1970 Nova Scotia and Prince Edward Island Acadians established their own organizations that received provincial support.

The establishment of a provincial organization in New Brunswick was not so easily accomplished. For nearly three years younger Acadian leaders clashed with the older elite, dubbed the Old Guard, over its formation. They sought direct confrontation with the province over the implementation of the school program in particular and bilingual services in general, something the older elite had never done.

The Old Guard could not reconcile itself to the new militancy in the ranks of the young activists. For years they had labored through the church and related institutions to develop Acadie. Their efforts culminated in the Robichaud reforms, but these in turn brought forth a new militancy advanced by a more vocal and active ethnic leadership that had been mobilized by the Old Guard, their ideology, their associations, and their schools. From the Old Guard's perspective they could not see that the Robichaud reforms fostered such a course of events because it altered the Acadian sector's relationship to the wider society.

In June 1973 a compromise of sorts was reached. The SANB was organized as a provincial pressure group led by the more pragmatic of the new leaders. It is funded completely by federal money. But the SNA would continue in existence in the background in the event federal funds were cut off. The Old Guard withdrew from the forefront of Acadian nationalism in 1973 and a new, more politically oriented leadership took over.

CONCLUSION

Although the Acadian ethnic nationalist movement has not reached the matured phase and may never reach it, its course of development shows a continuing response to the intrusion of the Canadian welfare state into local and community organization. At first mediated through a local ethnic elite, later through a provincial ethnic leadership, and finally by a ramified ethnic political pressure organization, the relationship of Acadian ethnic nationalism with the Canadian welfare state illustrates the nature of such movements as new forms of political mobilization in industrial societies.

Acadian ethnic nationalism serves as an illustration of the general developmental phases we believe ethnic nationalisms undergo. The Acadian situation also illustrates the factors we find to be causal in the emergence of ethnic nationalist movements, that is, the penetration of the welfare state into locality and community institutions, the challenge to local elites that such penetration presents, and the latter's organization of an ethnic political movement with which to limit, resist, or define state intrusion. Unlike alternative explanations that portray ethnic nationalisms as breakdowns in modernization or responses to internal colonialism or backward-looking ideologies, our perspective presents them as political responses, underwritten and manipulated by an ethnic leadership, to the most modernized form of society—the welfare state. In such societies ethnicity is more salient than socioeconomic class for the mobilization of a political following. Our treatment of ethnicity, at least as it appears in ethnic nationalism, is as an institution found in association with a particular form of the state. Our analysis therefore contextualizes ethnicity within the social institutions and political circumstances of the wider society.

NOTES

1. The research reported in this paper began in 1975 and is continuing. Aull, who is conducting field research in Wales, wishes to thank the Social Sciences Research Council Western European Program and the Wenner-Gren Foundation for aid. Cimino gratefully acknowledges the help of the Canadian Studies Program of Duke University in providing funds to undertake field research in New Brunswick. Grant SOC75-16593 from the National Science Foundation helped in the preliminary stages of this research.

2. Wolpe (1975) gives a specific and limited definition to the concept of internal colonialism by suggesting that it apply only to situations where an ethnic or social population is not fully integrated into the national economy (due to prejudice and exclusion) so that the population's economic output can be effectively exploited (at less cost to the economy than that required by the rest of the population). It would be difficult to characterize most ethnic populations in contemporary welfare states as internal colonies under this definition.

However, the argument could be made that contemporary welfare policies of modernized states perpetuate conditions of internal colonialism in economically marginal areas, whose labor product is still exploited by private enterprise. Whether this economic portrayal is true or not, the center of power shifts to the national or regional bureaucratic machinery, and protest movements like ethnic nationalism grow up in response to this political—rather than economic—situation.

3. Lipset's treatment of regionalism in northern Germany between the world wars as an extremist movement of the political center—the petty

businessmen, landowners, rentiers—does not adequately characterize present ethnic nationalist movements. The class-political categories of left, right, and center cannot be applied to such movements because they come into being in a period when these old ideological labels are more meaningful for the scholar than for the mobilization (and therefore scholarly interpretation) of political movements. However, see Lipset (1960 : 145) for a discussion of regionalist movements in class-political terms and for his objections to "the end of ideology" argument (pp. 403ff.).

4. New Brunswick has the highest percentage of Acadians of any of the Maritime provinces. Comparable figures for Prince Edward Island and Nova Scotia are less than 10 percent. In 1971 the Acadians represented 37 percent of the New Brunswick population compared to 13.7 percent for Prince Edward Island and 10.2 percent for Nova Scotia (Roy 1976).

5. Ten major conventions were held between 1881 and 1937. After that the national society remained dormant until 1957, when it was reconstituted as the Société Nationale des Acadiens.

REFERENCES

Barnett, Marguerite Ross, 1974. Creating Political Identity: The Emergent South Indian Tamils. *Ethnicity* 1 : 237–260.

Barth, Fredrik, ed., 1969. *Ethnic Groups and Boundaries*. (Boston: Little, Brown).

Baudry, René, 1966. Les Acadiens d'aujourd'hui. Rapport de recherche préparé pour la Commission royale d'enquête sur le bilinguilisme et le biculturalisme. Unpublished manuscript. Moncton: Centre d'études acadiennes.

Berger, Suzanne, n.d. Bretons and Jacobins: Reflections on French Regional Ethnicity. Unpublished manuscript prepared for Conference on Ethnic Pluralism and Conflict in Contemporary Western Europe and Canada, Center for International Studies, Cornell University.

Brass, Paul R., 1976. Ethnicity and Nationality Formation. *Ethnicity* 3 : 225–241.

Canada, Department of Forestry and Rural Development, 1966. *Northeast New Brunswick Federal Provincial Rural Development Agreement* (Ottawa: Queen's Printer).

Canada, Department of Regional Economic Expansion, 1972. *Northeast New Brunswick Federal Provincial Rural Development Agreement, as amended to September 5, 1972* (Ottawa: Queen's Printer).

Canada, Statistics Canada, 1941. *Census of Canada* (Ottawa: Queen's Printer).

Canadian Parliamentary Guide, 1873, 1875, 1879, 1883, 1887, 1891, 1897, 1903, 1909, 1914, 1917, 1920, 1926, 1931, 1936, 1940, 1945, 1949, 1953, 1957, 1961, 1963, 1968, 1971 (Ottawa: n.p.).

Cronin, Constance, 1970. *The Sting of Change* (Chicago: University of Chicago Press).

DeVos, George, 1975. Ethnic Pluralism: Conflict and Accommodation. In *Ethnic Identity*, George DeVos and Lola Romanucci-Ross, eds. (Palo Alto, Cal.: Mayfield Publishing).

Doucet, Camille-Antonio, 1973. *Une étoile s'est levée en Acadie* (Ottawa: Marcel François Richard). Les Editions du Renouveau.

Douglas, William A., and Milton da Silva, 1971. Basque Nationalism. In *The Limits of Integration: Ethnicity and Nationalism in Modern Europe*. Oriol Pi-Sunyer, ed. Research Reports 9. Department of Anthropology, University of Massachusetts, Amherst.

Eisenstadt, S. N., 1964 Breakdowns of Modernization. In *Readings in Social Evolution and Development*, S. N. Eisenstadt, ed. (Oxford: Pergamon Press).

Enloe, Cynthia, 1973. *Ethnic Conflict and Political Development* (Boston: Little Brown).

Even, Alan, 1970. Le territoire pilote du Nouveau-Brunswick ou les blocages culturels au développement économique. Contribution à une analyse socio-économique du développement (Ph.D. diss., Université de Rennes).

Gans, Herbert J., 1962. *Urban Villagers* (New York: Pree Press of Glencoe).

Gouldner, Alvin, 1970. *The Coming Crisis of Western Sociology* (New York and London: Basic Books).

Greenwood, Davydd J., 1975. The Emergence of Irreconcilable Differences: Spanish Basque Ethnicity as an Historical Process. Unpublished manuscript prepared for Conference on Ethnic Pluralism and Conflict in Contemporary Western Europe and Canada, Center for International Studies, Cornell University.

Hannerz, Ulf, 1974. Ethnicity and Opportunity in Urban America. In *Urban Ethnicity*, Abner Cohen, ed. (New York: Tavistock).

Hautecoeur, Jean-Paul, 1975. *L'Acadie du discours. Pour une sociologie de la culture acadienne* (Quebec: Les Presses de l'Université Laval).

Hechter, Michael, 1971. Toward a Theory of Ethnic Change. *Politics and Society* 2 : 21–45.

————, 1975. *Internal Colonialism. The Celtic Fringe in British National Development, 1536–1966* (Berkeley: University of California Press).

Keyes, Charles F., 1976. Towards a New Formulation of the Concept of Ethnic Group. *Ethnicity* 3 : 203–213.

Lipset, Seymour Martin, 1960. *Political Man* (Garden City, N.Y.: Doubleday).

Mailhot, Raymond, 1973. Prise de conscience collective acadienne au Nouveau-Brunswick, 1860–1890, et comportement de la majorité anglophone (Ph.D. diss., Université de Montréal).

————, 1976. Quelques éléments d'histoire économique de la prise de conscience acadienne, 1850–1891. *Société Historique Acadienne*, Cahiers 7 (2) : 49–74.

Nagata, Judith A., 1974. What is a Malay? Situational Selection of Ethnic Identity in a Plural Society. *American Ethnologist* 1 : 331–350.

New Brunswick, 1963. *Report of the Royal Commission on Finance and Municipal Taxation in New Brunswick* (Fredericton: n.p.).

Reiter, Rayna R., 1972. Modernization in the South of France: The Village and Beyond. *Anthropological Quarterly* 45(1) : 35–53.

Robidoux, Ferdinand, 1907. *Conventions Nationales des Acadiens: Recueil des Travaux et délibérations des six premiers conventions*, Vol. 1. (Shediac, N.B.: Le Moniteur Acadien).

Roy, Thérèse B., c.s.c., 1976. *Population totale et population acadienne des*

Provinces Maritimes de 1871 à 1971 (Moncton: Centre d'études aca-diennes).

Rumilly, Robert, 1955. *Histoire des Acadiens* (Montreal: Fides).

Sahlins, Marshall, 1976. *The Use and Abuse of Biology: An Anthropological Critique of Sociobiology* (Ann Arbor: University of Michigan Press).

Savoie, Alexandre-J., 1976. Une demi-siècle d'histoire acadienne (Montreal: l'Imprimerie Gagneltee.)

Stack, Carol, 1974. *All Our Kin: Strategies for Survival in a Black Community* (New York: Harper and Row).

Thorburn, Hugh G., 1961. *Politics in New Brunswick* (Toronto: University of Toronto Press).

Tomasi, Silvano M., and Madeline A. Engel, eds., 1970. *The Italian Experience in the United States* (Staten Island: Center for Migration Studies).

van den Berghe, Pierre L., n.d. Ethnic Pluralism in Industrial Societies: A Special Case? Unpublished manuscript prepared for the Conference on Ethnic Pluralism and Conflict in Contemporary Western Europe and Canada, May 1975. Western Societies Program, Center for International Studies, Cornell University.

Whalen, H. J., 1963. *The Development of Local Government in New Brunswick* (Fredericton, New Brunswick: n.p.).

Wolpe, Harald, 1975. The Theory of Internal Colonialism: The South African Case. In *Beyond the Sociology of Development: Economy and Society in Latin America and Africa*, Ivar Oxaal, Tony Barnett, and David Booth, eds. (London: Routledge and Kegan Paul Ltd.), pp. 229–252.

Discussion: Ethnicity and the State

MARY W. HELMS

Many writers have commented that ethnicity, which is associated with heterogeneous complex societies, is very widespread in time and space. It is "a ubiquitous phenomenon in both developing and developed countries, past and present" (Cohen 1974 : ix). Yet the formal study of ethnicity and the concept of ethnicity as a heuristic device are very young, at least among anthropologists, who are well advised that "the present state of comparative knowledge about ethnicity permits no more than a few empirical generalizations and cautious hypotheses" (van den Berghe 1976 : 244).

Virtually every scholarly report on ethnicity begins with an analytical definition of the phenomenon under consideration. These definitions focus on a number of characteristics associated with ethnicity and ethnic groups. The definitive qualities most frequently cited include a subjective sense on the part of ethnic group members of shared identity and of distinctness from other peoples. Distinctness is expressed in select cultural traditions or cultural "markers" of language, religion, nationality, race, and other points of reference by which ethnic consciousness is given material and symbolic form. Some scholars have extended this definition further, viewing ethnicity as an epistemological device by which cultural heterogeneity is ordered and people are categorized in terms of criteria of origin and background (Barth 1969; see discussion in Cohen 1974: xii–xv). Alternatively, it has been claimed that ethnic categories really operate more like roles and are "in that sense only very indirectly descriptive of the empirical characteristics of substantive groups of people" (Lehman 1967 : 107). In this view ethnic categories and identities are relative to situations, rather than being absolute structural units.

Still other writers, interested in those situations in which ethnicity occurs, stress its functions as a "rational group response to social pressures and a basis for concerted group action where none other exists" (Duran 1974 : 43). In these terms ethnicity is commonly considered an active political instrument basically concerned with the allocation of scarce (limited) resources (Barth 1969; van den Berghe 1976 : 250). Ethnicity, in fact, is all these things, as Cohen succinctly states when he says that "the cultures of ethnic groups are universes of . . . formally non-political formations and activities that are politicized in the course of social action" (1974 : xvi).

So many factors enter into the various expressions of ethnicity that ethnicity, however defined, appears to be relative to time and place (particularly if time and place are macroscopically considered), changing its form and function and varying in degree "with alternations in social structures and the climate of opinion . . ." (Schermerhorn 1974 : 2; Cohen 1974 : xv). Included among the social and ideological milieux that affect expressions of ethnicity are the perceived needs of the group, its size and distribution, its relationships with other groups, and the overall political context. This last item—political context—may be the most significant variable determining the form and function of ethnicity.

Ethnicity in general appears to be associated with complex heterogeneous societies, that is, with the state level of sociocultural integration. In this context, broadly speaking, an ethnic group or ethnic community "is an alternative form of social organization to class and ethnicity is an alternative form of identification to class consciousness" (Brass 1976: 226). As a general characteristic of states, it is also to be expected that some features of ethnicity (for example, the possibility that ethnic elites may try to manipulate ethnic populations for their own political advantage) will be common to most or all state forms at one time or another. In its more specific or diverse manifestations, however, various elements or expressions of ethnicity *may* be correlated with particular structural or organizational variants of state formation. Depending on the wider political circumstances, for example, expressions of ethnicity may involve only ethnic elites or they may involve the entire ethnic population; group members may be active as individuals or the group as a whole may be mobilized; ethnic activities may focus primarily on local affairs or may reach to the highest, federal level of government; interethnic relationships may be competitive or symbiotic in form. Consequently, in order to comprehend the nature and significance of specific manifestations of ethnicity, it is necessary to identify and understand the diverse structures and modes of operation of various state forms. Further, state forms should be considered both as individual polities and as members of larger, multistate or worldwide, political and economic systems or alliances (see Hechter 1976).

This point is particularly relevant for our times, for recent decades have witnessed a number of changes in contemporary state organizations that have been paralleled by significant expressions of ethnicity. To take two of the most obvious examples, internal readjustments have occurred within the political system of the United States such that the federal government has come to control a larger share of national resources than ever before and, as a result, has reached new heights of power. On the international front, the overseas colonial empires developed by industrializing nations of Western Europe over the course of the last several centuries have crumbled, producing a congeries of newly independent polities faced with the challenge of modernization and nation building. These developments have produced changes in the nature and expression of ethnicity in the contemporary United States and in the Third World, as several of the papers in this volume illustrate.

Let us consider Smith's intriguing discussion of the ill-fated Portuguese Day celebration in the New England town of Texton, by way of example. Smith has described how the community's political leaders' decision to honor the Old and New Portuguese who had settled in the town did not establish the anticipated harmony but instead led to increased tensions. We can understand the situation more clearly if we realize that the attitudes of Texton's Old and New Portuguese, respectively, are grounded in two distinct political-ideological eras in recent United States history. Furthermore, one of these, the laissez-faire industrializing order of the nineteenth century and first half of the twentieth century, has been increasingly overridden during the last decade or two in some important political respects by the other, the newly emergent bureaucratic welfare state.

If the United States experience can be taken as guide, the role of ethnicity and the position of ethnic groups in society differ significantly between advanced industrializing societies and bureaucratic welfare states. Briefly summarized, successful industrialization of the Western powers required a constant supply of unskilled and semiskilled labor at minimal cost. These needs were met most readily through the immigration of cheap labor from impoverished and culturally distinctive regions peripheral to the industrial core. Immigrant laborers were also forced to compete among themselves for jobs in the relatively small range of occupations deemed proper for them, and also were consigned, by virtue of their poverty, to residential segregation. Job competition, occupational and residential segregation, and cultural distinctiveness contributed to the establishment and maintenance of ethnic identities and ethnic communities in industrializing society (see Hechter 1976; Hannerz 1974).

At the same time, however, assimilationism was the dominant ideology of society at large. In the United States "popular opinion showed tolerance for European immigrants only when they were willing to give up their language and foreign customs; self-effacement was the price of acceptance. With few exceptions, the newcomers found it expedient to adopt this viewpoint and thus win their eligibility for the title 'American' " (Schermerhorn 1974 : 4). Americanization also seemed to have some basis in fact, for by 1950 many second-generation ethnic Americans had achieved an occupational level equal to that of the nation as a whole (ibid., p. 6).

During the 1960's, as is well known, significant changes appeared in the political ideology and political activities of ethnic groups. These adjustments were precipitated by the emergence of the federal government as the center of national power, and the gradual decline in unskilled and semiskilled jobs as technology advanced. For those in the lower economic and social sectors the best opportunities for social and economic improvement now lay in the largesse of the federal government. Consequently, competition among ethnic groups shifted from the local to the national level as ethnic communities jockeyed for a share of federal funds and programs. Concurrently the ideology of assimilation was superseded by the current ideology of cultural pluralism (Schermerhorn 1974; Glazer and Moynihan 1974).

The New England factory town of Texton was clearly caught up in this change. In earlier, more prosperous times Texton had been a thriving industrial center in which the local industrial elite enjoyed political prominence and exploited the labor of the Old Portuguese in the textile factories. More recently, however, this manufacturing base had fallen upon hard times. Yet even as local industry faltered, the New Portuguese were successfully tapping a new resource base of federal grants, which provided them with educational and occupational benefits unavailable to the Old Portuguese. Although Smith is not explicit on this point, it is likely that to the Old Portuguese ethnic identity had encouraged intragroup cohesion necessary for survival in the system of competitive and impersonal factory exploitation by which they lived. To the New Portuguese, however, ethnicity not only provided group identity and cohesion but, more important, it was a tool for active pursuit of resources. Ethnicity structured the intergroup relationships, linking them vertically with federal and state agencies dispensing benefits and tying them horizontally to even more recent Portuguese arrivals who needed community services which were being offered by entrepreneurial New Portuguese to still newer immigrants. There was no place for the already established third-generation Old Portuguese in this more recent political order. Their only hope of advancement lay in pursuing the assimilationist ideology congruent with "their era" and in seeking identification as Americans in order to merge (it was hoped) with the mainstream of American life.

Texton's industrial elite probably feared a similar obsolescence in the new bureaucratic-welfare state. Their reaction was to sponsor Portuguese

Day, hoping, I suspect, to reaffirm both to the community and to themselves that, in spite of the decline of the local industry on which they
traditionally had based their power and the increased power and resource
control of the central government, they were still a viable political force
on the local level. To make this point they, too, appealed to the assimilationist ideology of Americanization. By lumping all Portuguese together
and emphasizing that Portuguese contributions to Texton also made them
good Americans, the Texton elite may have been attempting a revival
of the industrial era ideology reminiscent of Texton's earlier and better
days when the town elite was still confident of its leadership position.

Alternatively, the Texton elite may not have been indulging in remem-
brances of things past but may have sensed a very contemporary need for
affirmation by all citizens of Texton of the community's viability in the
face of the growing federal influence in their lives. In this context the
only identification common to the multiethnic community which the
elite could emphasize was "American-ness." This identification suited
the Old Portuguese, who resented being labeled as ethnic, but not the
New Portuguese, who have found their ethnic identification useful politically. Division thus continued in the Portuguese community in spite
of the unity intended by a Portuguese Day celebration lauding good
Americans.

Another view of the role of ethnicity in the contemporary welfare
state is afforded us by Molina's discussion of the problems faced by community organizers in multiethnic neighborhoods. In his experience and
that reported by other community organizers, ethnicity benefits poor
minorities by giving them visibility that can be used to acquire service
program benefits from the government. However, Molina finds there may
be a limit to the organizational potential of ethnicity in this context.
While ethnically defined organization brings services to the population,
it may not automatically be further activated as a self-propelled political
force representing the poor.

It is pertinent to note here the emphasis by Fox, Aull, and Cimino on
the multisector characteristics of ethnic nationalist movements in contemporary welfare states and the important role of ethnic leaders—
generally of the middle class—in uniting hitherto separate or even antagonistic ethnic elements into common cause. In Molina's experience, however, community organization (which need not be the same type of
ethnic expression as ethnic nationalism) may be hampered by the potential inherent in ethnic populations to become themselves a political resource to be manipulated by politically ambitious local leaders for the
leaders' benefit (as the industrial elite of Texton apparently tried to do).
When this occurs, as it frequently has in many state forms, past and

present (see Brass 1976), ethnic populations may find that they have not really gained an active voice in political affairs. To achieve this goal they must be reidentified by their political leaders as active interest groups rather than as passive population aggregates for elite use. But Molina notes that in multiethnic neighborhoods, cultural differences in identification of necessary action-steps and the fissioning quality inherent in multiethnicity as an organizational principle make it difficult to rise beyond ethnic closure and to develop the pluralistic alliances necessary for the development of this more positive political role. This problem is common to much of contemporary America, not only for individual neighborhoods but for the nation as a whole. It is the opinion of more than one observer that, while pluralistic alliance could best provide the necessary pressures for greater social justice in the United States, it is less likely to be realized than other ethnic trends toward polarization or proliferation, which eventually could have more disastrous consequences for all (see Schermerhorn 1974 : 10–13).

To date the political benefits—as well as the shortcomings—of multiethnic alliances may be best studied in the pluralistic societies of the Third World. The circumstances of emerging nationhood in which ethnicity is found here, however, should not automatically be considered directly comparable to the political and economic contexts in which ethnicity exists in well-established industrialized nation-states, though analogous circumstances can be found in specific instances, such as competition for unskilled jobs in the cities. For one thing, the greater ethnic heterogeneity—that is, the much greater percentage of the total population which actively utilizes ethnicity as an organizational-behavioral form in Third World pluralistic societies—not only reflects differences in political-economic structures between industrialized and newly developing states, but also sometimes creates differences of degree in the expression of ethnicity that may become differences in kind when compared to ethnicity in industrialized states.

In the introduction to his analysis of Indian and Pakistani workers in London, for example, Gumperz briefly compares and contrasts the nature of contacts between ethnic members and government officers or elites in pluralistic societies and in industrial-welfare states. In the former case, ego's relationships with officialdom may be limited in context and mediated by specialists in intergroup communication. In the latter, contacts between ethnics and officials are greatly widened in context, but effective mediators are lacking. Other contrasts in terms of the nature of ethnic groups (e.g., the number of groups in a society, their relative size, their degree of geographical separation, the degree of individual mobility among groups) and the type and range of institutional expressions of power and production may be anticipated (see van den Berghe 1973: 968–969).

The origins of contemporary ethnicity in postcolonial plural societies is another point of contrast and comparison. In Africa, for example (as well as in other Third World nations), ethnicity may be interpreted both as traditional and as newly emergent. In some instances multiethnic ("tribal") situations that were socially and economically useful prior to European colonialism were given further support by colonial governments and policies and have continued into the postcolonial era where they have received new impetus and intensification by forces of modernization and urbanization. "The political independence of 'new nations' has often led both to a drive for national unity and to a perception of tribal division apparently sharper than in the years of colonial overrule" (Charsley 1974 : 337). In other circumstances—or in the opinions of other observers—"most of the so-called 'tribalism' that bedevils African life at the present time is a recent growth" generated by forces and reorganizations of nationalism and modernization, by the growth of new states with new political roles, and by the intrusion of the state into areas of local and personal life formerly controlled by communities and the individual (Colson 1974 : 103, 104).

Ethnicity as traditional or newly emergent may also reflect rural and urban adaptations, respectively.

> In rural Africa, tribal identity persists because the colonial government gave it an institutional and political support and because the tie to the tribal, communal, or lineage land, often phrased in the idiom of filial loyalty to ancestors, is still an important social and economic asset. In the urban area, factors contributing to ethnic loyalty include the competition for jobs, the uneven distribution of government patronage, and the insecurity of urban employment. There is also an element of "ethnic patriotism"—an important value which conflicts with a wider national loyalty. (Uchendu 1975 : 269)

Unfortunately, ethnic loyalty and "patriotism" not infrequently have generated serious conflict and violence when preferred jobs or key political positions or socially prestigious roles were held by members of some ethnic groups more than by others. This inequality compels ethnic interests to compete both for defense of their perceived interests and for further development of interests, for accommodation or domination within the developing state (cf. Duran 1974).

These generalizations point to some of the processes involving ethnicity in contemporary Africa. Many questions, however, remain to be answered, not the least of which asks why some groups develop processes of ethnicity more than others and whether economic and/or political factors are always primary in these decisions (see Charsley 1974). Political and economic interests do seem to underlie the ethnic situation in northern Tanzania discussed by Guillotte. Here, in a hinterland region, local ethnic groups act as politically significant interest groups. In fact, Guillotte notes that in developing Third World states such as Tanzania, where national political leaders are still struggling to extend nation-oriented ties and identity to the population at large and still have only partial control over national resources (see Fallers 1974 : 31–69), ethnicity may be perceived by nation-builders as a rival political system (see also Colson 1974 : 105). Certainly for well-entrenched and rather immobile groups such as the Mbugwe and for small groups such as the Barabaig, maintenance of ethnic distinctions (in this case by use of tribal language as an ethnic point of reference) may effectively limit the extent of government interference in their affairs and allow a measure of political independence, social distance, and protection of resources.

The Swahili speakers of Magugu, in contrast, have cast their lot, for better or for worse, with the national political organization. They have been forced to do so because the plethora of linguistic and tribal identities open to them as a population aggregate obviates the political usefulness of ethnicity. The divisiveness of the multitude of ethnic units that would emerge if tribal identity or languages were emphasized in Magugu would far outweigh the benefits of this ethnic unity. Such divisiveness would render the population politically helpless. Ethnicity, in short, has its limitations as a political instrument. Sufficient population size and density within a given territory must exist for ethnicity to be helpful as an organizing principle. Failing this, another organizational point of reference—such as national identification—may be the better or perhaps the only political expedient for the population of a local territory.

In casting their lot with the national political organization, in stressing identity via citizenship over identity by ethnicity, the Swahili speakers of Kibaoni and Magugu appear to resemble the Old Portuguese of Texton, who also have opted for identification via national citizenship over that of ethnicity, although for quite a different reason. By opting for national citizenship, both the Old Portuguese and the people of Magugu must give up whatever political clout accrues to those of their neighbors who prefer to (or must) seek political goals via ethnicity. It should also be noted that the function of ethnicity contrasts significantly with these neighbors, i.e., the New Portuguese of Texton and the Mbugwe and Barabaig of northern Tanzania. The New Portuguese are seeking access to resources controlled and distributed by a powerful federal government while the Mbugwe and Barabaig are seeking to protect already acquired resources which they fear may be lost to them as the central government expands its controls. In order to achieve these contrasting goals, both the New Portuguese of Texton and the Mbugwe and Barabaig of Tanzania find (or hope to find) the necessary room to maneuver by using ethnic identity to create social distance between themselves and the wider society. On the other hand, when and if their ends may be better served by reducing social distance, the Mbugwe and Barabaig readily stress ties of citizenship. Ethnicity, as a number of writers have argued, often appears to be situational (role-like) rather than structural (categorical) in nature, particularly, although by no means exclusively, in developing countries such as Tanzania in which self-identification by ethnicity can offer a viable alternative identification (not only a second identification) to that by citizenship (see Lehman 1967).

In this context one wishes for more information concerning how leaders of linguistically differentiated populations such as the Mbugwe, Barabaig, and Magugu comprehend in their own *emic* terms the complexity and subtlety of differential linguistic intelligibility. Lieberson has set forth some of these linguistic situations in formal, algebraic terms, but the influences on communication of mother tongue composition, bilingualism, and segregation apparently are also well understood by the ethnic leaders of Tanzanian groups, who deftly manipulate these aspects of linguistic diversity for their political advantage and that of their constituents. Such understanding undoubtedly plays an important role in supporting and strengthening the position of ethnic leaders as power-brokers and can be considered part of the specialized knowledge that such leaders must develop if they are to be successful. The elegance of Lieberson's algebraic determinations would probably be lost upon them, but the practical effects of the various linguistic circumstances Lieberson investigates would be well appreciated.

French's discussion of missionaries and the Eastern Cherokee turns our attention to the active colonial expansionism pursued by the industrializing powers of the Northern Hemisphere over the last four hundred years. During these centuries, indeed, throughout the thousands of years since the initial evolution of states, the frontiers or hinterlands of state territories have offered rich material for ethnic studies. In these circumstances ethnicity can be observed both in the divisions that occurred among contact agents, such as missionaries or traders, working in the hinterland and in the development of so-called colonial or secondary tribes (of which the postcontact Eastern Cherokee are an example).

Secondary tribes come about in several ways. Active resistance on the part of indigenous peoples to the geographical expansion of the state may create new tribal or ethnic organization in state hinterlands. "Indeed, states with somewhat greater sophistication may create tribes as a means of ordering the areas immediately beyond the territories being directly ruled" (Fried 1975 : 101). They can also arise as a consequence of the state's economic expansion. The central polity, demanding tribute, in effect creates or encourages new forms of organization in the less-developed societies to facilitate the wealth-taking. Nonofficial (nonpolitical) economic contacts may also encourage the emergence of new organizations and new tribal (ethnic) identifications, as when trade routes are extended across the country, opening opportunities for middlemen positions or plunder (Fried 1975 : 102; Helms 1969). Finally, "it is even possible, though I have no cases to cite, that tribes could appear as the result of ideological pressures. Thus it is conceivable that missionaries would forge such units to facilitate their task of conversion, or merely because they could not see the nonstate world except as comprised of tribes, so manufactured them to fulfill their own expectations" (Fried 1975 : 102).

Whether or not missionaries have ever created secondary tribes to facilitate their work, it does appear that the mission community itself is frequently characterized by tight in-group cohesion and fierce intergroup conflict among the members of the various churches who seek souls to be saved in the hinterland. Indeed, one is led to suspect that the missionizing process strongly encourages such interdenominational conflict (it may be inherent in missionization) as a means of increasing the solidarity and sharpening the self-identity of the respective mission communities involved. This rivalry also can be interpreted in ecological terms as multiethnic (denominational) competition for scarce resources (native membership in the respective frontier churches). Often, however, the spread of the Gospel is hindered more than helped by mission competitions, as bewildered natives have frequently noted themselves.

Isolated state hinterlands may also provide places of refuge where minority or fundamentalist mission groups—in the situation discussed by French, the Baptists, Methodists, Moravians, and Quakers of the earlier Appalachian frontier—may feel freer to live their lives and express their beliefs, being removed from the pressures of the larger cosmopolitan society where they may have to assume a more defensive position in the presence of other "majority" or "elite" religions. If such is the case, in order to properly understand the role of missions in colonial frontiers, we must also consider the position of the home church in the heartland (for example see Gollin 1967; Helms 1971 : 239–250). Also significant, as French has indicated, is the manner in which the effects of the state's attempts to exploit the hinterland (in this case a reduction of agricultural land brought about by tourist-oriented enterprises) and to establish its ideological superiority may be expressed by (or reflected in) mission conflicts. This being the case, it appears quite likely that the particular expressions of mission ethnicity that may occur in various circumstances may be influenced, at least in part, by the type of state with which the particular missions are involved. French's paper is particularly valuable for the data provided on this point, all the more so because such studies are too few.

In Fried's opinion, the concept of secondary tribalism as a phenomenon directly associated with the imperialism of the state can assist in our understanding of diverse political developments of our time, including "the continuation of ethnic hostility and actual warfare within modern states in Europe and elsewhere, and the apparently rising tide of separatism, within the context of single unitary states, of diverse 'ethnic groups'" (Fried 1975:104). This observation brings us to the discussion by Fox, Aull, and Cimino of ethnic nationalism in industrial societies.

Fox and his coauthors see ethnic nationalism as a local-level response to the increased puissance and intrusion of the welfare state, which controls the major sources of power and which gravely affects local-level affairs by its policies. Not surprisingly, some (though not all) ethnic nationalist movements occur in locales of rising wealth and industrial development, indicating that the leaders of such movements, and perhaps also some of their followers, are particularly fearful of losing access to the resources that would underwrite their own opportunities for wealth and their prestigious position as local leaders and elite power-brokers. On a broader plane, however, ethnic nationalism may at least be attempted if the authority base (whatever that may be) of the traditional ethnic or regional elite is seriously threatened by a powerful central government.

Whether or not such separatist movements are likely to be successful is a question still to be resolved in many cases. Brass (1976:239), for one, is of the opinion that the present world system is highly unfavorable to secessionist strategies. He argues in effect that, given the great power of the welfare states within whose borders ethnic nationalism currently rises, successful secessionist movements require intervention on their behalf by external polities of comparable power. Such escalation, he argues, is not of interest to the major world powers today, who basically prefer to maintain stability in their relationships and to avoid really threatening intervention in each others' affairs, particularly if such interference could lead to direct confrontation.

The danger in the ethnic nationalist movements of our times, however, lies in the possibility of accidents and incidents that could nonetheless bring such confrontation about. Leaders of ethnic nationalist movements —particularly the newer, more radical brand of leadership which, as Fox et al. note, is not adverse to acts of subversion or violence—might well overtly attempt to force political escalation to bring attention to their claims and to achieve their goals. Depending on the circumstances of particular situations, escalation could, in fact, result. The consequences of the confrontations that might then ensue could be extremely serious.

My comments have emphasized the sociopolitical setting in which interethnic communication may occur more than the structure of communication channels or the nature or content of the information exchanges, subjects around which this volume has been directly oriented and which most of the contributors explicitly discuss. Cultural setting, of course, is an essential element in the communication process, as virtually all of the studies presented here have illustrated one way or another. The cultural heterogeneity characteristic of all forms of state societies makes states perfect laboratories for communication studies. There is good reason to think that as such studies continue they will cast new light both on communication processes and on the various economic, political, and ideological structures and operations characteristic of the several forms in which states occur.

I see this latter development, the identification and clarification of the various types of state societies, as particularly important for scholarly investigation of ethnicity. At our present state of knowledge, the concept of ethnicity covers many things. The term is a broad one, comparable in its breadth of application to the traditional anthropological concept of tribe. In coming years we may hope to develop greater rigor in the use of both the term *ethnic* and the concept of ethnicity. This growing sophistication, however, will require greater understanding of the economic and political (power) milieux in which ethnicity operates. Therefore, we must interweave specific studies of ethnic situations with investigation of the state level of sociocultural integration in all its diverse forms, past and present.

REFERENCES

Barth, Frederik, 1969. *Ethnic Groups and Boundaries* (Boston: Little, Brown).

Brass, Paul R., 1976. Ethnicity and Nationality Formation. *Ethnicity* 3 : 225–241.

Charsley, S. R., 1974. The Formation of Ethnic Groups. In *Urban Ethnicity*, Abner Cohen, ed. (London: Tavistock), pp. 337–368.

Cohen, Abner, 1974. Introduction: The Lesson of Ethnicity. In *Urban Ethnicity*, Abner Cohen, ed. (London: Tavistock), pp. ix–xxiv.

Colson, Elizabeth, 1974. *Tradition and Contract: The Problem of Order* (Chicago: Aldine).

Duran, James J., 1974. The Ecology of Ethnic Groups from Kenyan Perspective. *Ethnicity* 1 : 43–64.

Fallers, Lloyd A., 1974. *The Social Anthropology of the Nation-State* (Chicago: Aldine).

Fried, Morton H., 1975. *The Notion of Tribe* (Menlo Park, Cal.: Cummings).

Glazer, Nathan, and Daniel P. Moynihan, 1974. Why Ethnicity? *Commentary* (October): 33–39.

Gollin, Gillian L., 1967. *Moravians in Two Worlds* (New York: Columbia University Press).

Hannerz, Ulf, 1974. Ethnicity and Opportunity in Urban America. In *Urban Ethnicity*, Abner Cohen, ed. (London: Tavistock), pp. 37–76.

Hechter, Michael, 1976. Ethnicity and Industrialization: On the Proliferation of the Cultural Division of Labor. *Ethnicity* 3 : 214–224.

Helms, Mary W., 1969. The Cultural Ecology of a Colonial Tribe. *Ethnology* 8 : 76–84.

———, 1971. *Asang: Adaptations to Culture Contact in a Miskito Community* (Gainesville: University of Florida Press).

Lehman, F. K., 1967. Ethnic Categories of Burma and the Theory of Social Systems. In *Southeast Asian Tribes, Minorities, and Nations*, Peter Kunstadter, ed. (Princeton: Princeton University Press), pp. 93–124.

Schermerhorn, R. A., 1974. Ethnicity in the Perspective of the Sociology of Knowledge. *Ethnicity* 1 : 1–14.

Uchendu, Victor C., 1975. The Dilemma of Ethnicity and Polity Primacy in Black Africa. In *Ethnic Identity, Cultural Continuities and Change*, George De Vos and Lola Romanucci-Ross, eds. (Palo Alto, Cal.: Mayfield), pp. 265–275.

van den Berghe, Pierre L., 1973. Pluralism. In *Handbook of Social and Cultural Anthropology*, John J. Honigmann, ed. (Chicago: Rand McNally), pp. 959–977.

———, 1976. Ethnic Pluralism in Industrial Societies: A Special Case? *Ethnicity* 3 : 242–255.

The Contributors

CHARLOTTE AULL is a candidate for the Ph.D. in Anthropology at Duke University. She has done fieldwork in Wales on ethnic political movements.

LOUIS CIMINO has done fieldwork on ethnic nationalism in French Canada. He is a candidate for the Ph.D. in Anthropology at Duke University.

RICHARD G. FOX is Professor of Anthropology at Duke University. His primary interests are in urban anthropology and in the anthropology of political systems. He is presently the editor of the *American Ethnologist*.

LAWRENCE FRENCH is a member of the faculty of the Department of Criminal Justice at the University of Nebraska. He has worked among the Eastern Cherokee in North Carolina both as a change agent and as a researcher.

JOSEPH V. GUILLOTTE III is Associate Professor of Anthropology at the University of New Orleans. His major research focus is on Sub-Saharan Africa. His most recent research in Tanzania concentrated on social integration in a multiethnic rural community.

JOHN J. GUMPERZ, Professor of Anthropology at the University of California at Berkeley, has been a leader in sociolinguistic studies since the 1950's. His research areas are India, Europe, and the urban United States. He is coeditor of *Directions in Socio-linguistics: The Ethnography of Communication*.

MARY HELMS is Lecturer in Anthropology at Northwestern University. Her primary area of interest is culture change in state hinterlands, especially Central America. She has authored *Middle America* and *Asang* and has coauthored *Frontier Adaptations in Lower Central America*.

STANLEY LIEBERSON is Professor of Sociology at the University of Arizona. His main interests are sociolinguistics and ethnic relations. He is the author of "A Societal Theory of Race and Ethnic Relations" and *Language and Ethnic Relations in Canada*.

JOSÉ M. MOLINA is Adjunct Professor of Community Services, Miami Dade Community College. He also serves as director of All Peoples' Neighborhood Organization, sponsored by Christian Community Service Agency, Inc., in Miami, Florida. A native of Honduras, he has an M.A. degree from the University of Northern Colorado.

E. LAMAR ROSS is Assistant Professor of Anthropology at Florida International University. He has done fieldwork in New Orleans, Puerto Rico, and India. His current research interest is in interethnic communication.

M. ESTELLIE SMITH is Professor of Anthropology at the State University of New York at Oswego. Her research interests include ethnic enclaves, urban anthropology, ethnolinguistics, and the theory of cultural stability and change.

FATHI S. YOUSEF is Associate Professor of Communication Studies in the Department of Speech Communication, California State University, Long Beach. He received his M.A. in Linguistics and Anthropology and his Ph.D. in Communication and Business Administration from the University of Minnesota. He is coauthor of *An Introduction to Intercultural Communication.*